D1567650

— 150 — HOTELS
YOU NEED
TO VISIT BEFORE
— YOU DIE —

By Debbie Pappyn,
Travel Journalist at
Classe Touriste.

Lannoo

OVERVIEW

OVERVIEW

OVERVIEW

Introduction

By Debbie Pappyn, *Classe Touriste*

There's something eternally magical about pushing open the door of a new hotel room in expectation of what awaits on the other side – the novelty, the surprise, the views, the fragrance of crisp bed linen, the soft sound of the welcome tune on loop on the TV. After trying out well over a thousand different hotels during a lifetime of travelling around the world, I've always loved this moment and am perhaps even addicted to it. It's all about that feeling of arrival in a temporary home. Maybe it's a canvas yurt in a remote meadow somewhere in Mongolia, or a luxury suite behind a heavy, sound-proofed door in a Park Hyatt in some cosmopolitan, bright-lights city, a door that separates the frantic world out there from the calm, silent retreat inside. Hotels are worlds in miniature, different worlds, worlds endowed with singular rules and pleasures, places where falling asleep and waking are so different from at home. Maybe there's the sound of the ocean out back, like in Room 28 at the Wickaninnish Inn on Vancouver Island, or the whisper of reeds at the Inle Princess Resort in Burma, or the hippos laughing away after dusk, just like that night I spent at San Camp.

Often, it's not about the out-and-out luxuries like the gold taps, the over-the-top service and crazy amenities. Great hotels come in different shapes and sizes. Take the charming Haus Hirt inn in Austria: I would book a stay here in a jiff just to enjoy the wonderful long-drawn-out organic breakfast with a panoramic view over the snow-capped Alps. Or the Four Seasons Park Lane in London where I could stay in bed all day and night. Hotel beds can be absolute bliss, but there's always the danger that you'll never want to leave the room and go out and explore. 'Do not disturb' signs are a hotel lover's best friend. From the glorious beds, gourmet breakfasts, and views to die for, to the miniature shampoo bottles that you take home and use to help you travel back to a place in your imagination whenever you feel nostalgic… hotels are pure romance. Hotels tell stories. Hotels make stories and create memories. Enjoy these 150 places to stay, and don't forget to switch on the 'DND' on your smartphone!

— 01 —
SAN CAMP

| BOTSWANA | Kalahari Desert | LEGENDARY |
| | Makgadikgadi | TENTED CAMP |

◆ TO VISIT BEFORE YOU DIE BECAUSE
This camp is the epitome of romance and style in Africa.

With views over the shimmering salt pans of the Makgadikgadi, San Camp is a cluster of pure-white tents set amid grassland – the ultimate, romantic African hideaway. The spacious, light-filled tents are stocked with museum–worthy antiques and collectables from the old days when the owner's father, Jack Bousfield, was a record-breaking hunter and safari pioneer in Africa.

The communal spaces are equally chic and classic, with fine linen and delicate tableware used during long and relaxing lunches between game drives and explorations of this remote corner of Botswana.

€€€€
From €1,120 / US$1,260 per person per night, all inclusive.

MIGRANTE GUESTHOUSE

| CAPE VERDE | **Boa Vista** | COLONIAL |
| | Sal Rei | ISLAND VIBE |

◆ TO VISIT BEFORE YOU DIE BECAUSE

These islands are still a well-kept secret, with this small hotel as the ultimate must-stay.

Even though Cape Verde is today receiving more mainstream tourist attention, the island of Boa Vista and the little town of Sal Rei remain blissfully relaxed. Migrante Guesthouse has been here for well over two decades and is hidden in a colonial house situated in the old part of town. There are only five modest, yet comfortable rooms, each with its own distinctive personality and with lots of African and colonial charm, from creaky, wooden floors to four-poster beds. Downstairs there's an intimate courtyard with high, white walls and tall trees, the perfect spot for enjoying a long breakfast or reading a book before heading to the long and empty sand beaches, just a short stroll away from the hotel.

€
From €80 / US$90 per night for a double room, with breakfast.

www.migrante-guesthouse.com

SOFITEL LEGEND
OLD CATARACT ASWAN

EGYPT

Aswan
Banks of the River Nile

LEGENDARY
WRITER'S RETREAT

◆ TO VISIT BEFORE YOU DIE BECAUSE

This is the ultimate colonial grande dame of Northern Africa.

In this opulent hotel you may well stay in a room that has been occupied by Aga Khan III, the Shah of Iran, Princess Diana or Agatha Christie, as is evident from the hallways decked with photos of royals, artists and other VIPs who've bedded down here. This iconic hotel overlooks Elephantine Island at the crossroads of the Nile river valley and the Nubian Desert. The style is a mix of art deco and Mamluk glamour with a decor echoing ancient Egyptian motifs with a dash of French chic. When you check into the Old Cataract, you're stepping into an atmosphere reminiscent of an Agatha Christie tale, combined with an *English Patient* aura of a bygone era in North Africa.

€
From €120 / US$135 per night.

https://sofitel.accor.com/en/hotels/1666.html

— 04 —
KINONDO KWETU

| KENYA | Kinondo
Diani Beach | AFRICAN-CHIC
BEACH RETREAT |

◆ TO VISIT BEFORE YOU DIE BECAUSE

This is probably the best-kept secret along the Kenyan coast.

Book a room here and it will feel like you are staying in the private home of its owners, Ida and Filip Andersson, and their three children, a Swedish family related to the famous Baron Blixen. This intimate hotel, just south of Diani Beach, is a far cry from the big, impersonal resorts along the Kenyan coast. The private beach is calm with almost no outsiders passing by, the ocean is warm and blue, and the hotel has an intimate, cosy home-away-from-home feel, where like-minded guests come together to relax after a long safari trip. Highlights are dining on locally caught fish next to one of the two swimming pools with the Indian Ocean as a backdrop.

€€
From €210 / US$570 per person per night,
all inclusive.

— 05 —
LA MAMOUNIA

MOROCCO	**Marrakech**	PALACE RETREAT
	Medina	IN A SEA OF GREEN

◆ TO VISIT BEFORE YOU DIE BECAUSE
No other hotel can match its *Arabian Nights* vibe.

When celebs go on a romantic break to Marrakech, they hide away in the lush gardens of the iconic La Mamounia. There's no a more authentic way to enter a hotel in Morocco than being greeted by the typically dressed bell boys who lead you into a fairytale world of opulent decor with extravagant mosaics, hand-carved woodwork and sumptuous fabrics. The best buffet breakfast in town in served by the large outdoor pool, surrounded by lush, mature gardens. Rooms are intimate, some with views over the Koutoubia Mosque and the Atlas Mountains, while the villas in the garden are the ultimate hideaway for romantic weekends.

€€€
From €550 / US$620 per person per night.

— 06 —
SCARABEO CAMP

MOROCCO

Stone Desert
Agafay

CONTEMPORARY
DESERT ENCAMPMENT

◆ TO VISIT BEFORE YOU DIE BECAUSE

This is undoubtedly the most Instagrammable desert camp in the world.

Just a short drive from Marrakech, hidden in the vast Agafay Desert, sits Scarabeo 'Stone Desert' Camp with wide-open views of the Atlas Mountains. Fifteen luxurious and stylish nomad tents are strewn across an endless sea of desert, lit at night by hundreds of flickering lanterns. There's no better way to relax after a couple of days on the raucous streets of Marrakech than to sit on your porch with a glass of freshly brewed mint tea and inhale the vastness of the Agafay.

€€€€
From €1,120 / US$1,255 per person per night, all inclusive.

— 07 —
VILLA MABROUKA

MOROCCO	Strait of Gibraltar	ECCENTRIC
	Tangier	OASIS

◆ TO VISIT BEFORE YOU DIE BECAUSE

Everybody should stay at least once in a former residence of Yves Saint Laurent.

Famed British designer Jasper Conran bought the last private home of Yves Saint Laurent and his partner Pierre Bergé in Tangier, Morocco, and transformed it into an intimate hotel. The goal was to evoke 1930s charm while maintaining a timeless elegance. The 12-room hotel (each room is named after a Moroccan city) has been meticulously restored from a stunning 1940s modernist villa and boasts a truly unique location: the vibrant city of Tangier with its blend of European and African influences. Hidden within Tangier's grandest of gardens, Villa Mabrouka is a secret hideaway with a stunning courtyard full of banana and palm trees giving way to a giant garden, a true oasis of big, sweeping lawns looking out across the shimmering sea and filled with hollyhocks, giant rose bushes, lush bougainvillea, palm trees, perfumed jasmine and orange blossom. Inside the villa there are ornate wooden doors that swap the tropical, paradisiacal ambience for a cool and elegant decor filled with unique antiques. There's also a beautiful onsite restaurant and bar plus a spa with a traditional hammam.

€€€
From €405 for a double room with breakfast.

www.villamabrouka.com

NAMIBIA	Himba Land	SPLENDID
	Kunene River	ISOLATION

◆ TO VISIT BEFORE YOU DIE BECAUSE

It feels like staying at the edge of the world in a wonderful and comfy safari camp

Here you will hear the sound of the rushing water of the mighty Kunene river but close by, too, is also the driest desert in the world where the semi-nomadic Himba community live. Set under lush trees on the banks of the Kunene River, Serra Cafema is one of the most far-flung safari camps in Southern Africa. The eight cabins are set on elevated decks and crafted in wood, canvas and thatch to create a distinctive camp that blends into this remote, natural environment. The Ozonganda, or 'main area', offers mighty views over the river where little boat outings are possible, and Angola lies just on the other side of the water.

€€€
From €430 / US$480 per person per night, all inclusive.

NAMIBIA	**NamibRand** Namib Desert	THE SUPERLATIVE DESERT SANCTUARY EXPERIENCE

◆ TO VISIT BEFORE YOU DIE BECAUSE

This is the most iconic camp in Namibia, far from the busy tourist trail.

Just a few hours' drive from touristy and crowded Sossusvlei and hidden amid 220,000 hectares of the Namib Desert sits Wolwedans, a pioneer in sustainable and low-carbon footprint safari tourism. The privately owned and protected NamibRand is a swathe of unspoiled, red dune desert where Wolwedans offers a collection of singular wilderness camps and experiences. Come here for the emptiness and vastness of the Namib Desert, its dark skies and intense sunsets, without seeing other travellers. Dunes Lodge is the main camp while Boulders Camp has recently been revamped with a lavish swimming pool looking out over the massive granite rocks and red landscape.

€€€
From €410 / US$460 per person per night,
all inclusive.

150 HOTELS YOU NEED TO VISIT BEFORE YOU DIE

SINGITA KWITONDA LODGE

RWANDA

Volcanoes National Park
Sabyinyo views

A SANCTUARY
IN THE MIST

◆ TO VISIT BEFORE YOU DIE BECAUSE

This is the most beautiful safari lodge in the heart of Africa's gorilla territory.

Right on the edge of the enigmatic Volcanoes National Park, Singita Kwitonda Lodge is probably the first real luxury lodge for gorilla trekking enthusiasts in Rwanda. The lodge prioritises conservation but also offers a serious dose of creature – read: luxury – comfort. The decor brings together beautiful Rwandan culture and design, with woven ceilings and hand-fired terracotta that reflect local artistry. There are only seven suites – a perfect number for a safari lodge – all with private balconies overlooking the amazing scenery of the Sabyinyo, Gahinga and Muhabura volcanoes. After a memorable gorilla trekking adventure – and possible encounter – in the lush forest with Singita's expert guides, retreating to these suites is bliss: think indoor and outdoor showers, an indoor bath, a relaxing sitting area, and even a heated plunge pool, perfect for one of those chilly, après-safari evenings in the mountainous heart of Rwanda.

€€€€
From €1,700 / US$1,852 per person, all inclusive (including activities).

SEYCHELLES

Fregate
Four degrees south of the equator

MARINE
PARADISE

◆ TO VISIT BEFORE YOU DIE BECAUSE

Of all the exclusive private islands in the Seychelles this one has the most breathtaking natural beauty.

This little speck of granite is one of 115 islands in the Seychelles archipelago, blessed with seven spectacular and secluded beaches where endangered hawksbill turtles climb ashore to nest, and guests can hide away from the world. The 16 villas are built into the slopes of the island and are linked to the harbour and restaurant by forest trails. Each villa has a private infinity pool, a rainforest shower, unlimited privacy and views over the Indian Ocean.

€€€€
From €3,200 / US$3,590 a night in a villa, all inclusive, including buggy and activities.

— 12 —
HILTON SEYCHELLES NORTHOLME RESORT & SPA

SEYCHELLES

Glacis
Mahé Island

**CREOLE
WRITER'S DEN**

◆ TO VISIT BEFORE YOU DIE BECAUSE

This is the real Seychelles where you can meet the locals on white beaches and still stay in style.

The grande dame of the Seychelles is the Northolme Resort & Spa, where James Bond author Ian Fleming wrote a few of his bestsellers and enjoyed the local Mahé vibe while bathing in luxury and comfort. Northolme is adults-only (13+ years-old), so it is blissfully quiet and surrounded by rocks and huge granite boulders seen from the 56 treehouse-style villas that all look out over the Indian Ocean. Some villas have large infinity pools, and all are decorated in a warm, Creole style with lots of dark wood and bright-coloured accents.

€€
From €350 / US$390 a night with breakfast.

| SOUTH AFRICA | **The Winelands** | CAPE TOWN |
| | Groot Drakenstein Valley | FARM CHIC HOTEL |

◆ TO VISIT BEFORE YOU DIE BECAUSE

Experience the essence of the oldest Cape Dutch farm in the Winelands.

Babylonstoren feels like a never-ending oasis in the middle of a spectacular valley with the Simonsberg, Du Toitskloof and Franschhoek mountains as a majestic backdrop. This 200-hectare (500-acre) farm dates back to 1692 and features an impressive fruit, herb and vegetable garden next to a cool rural hotel and spa. Some of the old farm buildings have been transformed into sophisticated hotel rooms and suites. Housed in the homestead's original cowshed, Babel is the laid-back, yet chic bistro serving simple dishes with local ingredients, in a setting that is a wonderful blend of Cape Dutch architecture and contemporary decor.

€€€
From €420 / US$470 per night in B&B with extra amenities in the room.

LEKKERWATER BEACH LODGE

| SOUTH AFRICA | Western Cape | BEACHFRONT |
| | De Hoop Nature Reserve | HIDEAWAY |

◆ TO VISIT BEFORE YOU DIE BECAUSE

You will have the Indian Ocean all to yourself.

Lekkerwater means 'good water' in Afrikaans and this is exactly what you will get when you drive three-and-a-half hours from Cape Town to this very remote corner of De Hoop Nature Reserve. There seems to be hardly another a living soul in this protected stretch of marine reserve, where fynbos vegetation dominates the spectacular views. There are only seven rooms along a 6-kilometre (4-mile) stretch of private beach where whales and dolphins can be spotted during the winter season. Lekkerwater is South Africa's ultimate, secret beach getaway, where you won't have to share the ocean with anyone else.

€€
From €180 / US$200 per person, all inclusive.

www.naturalselection.travel/camps/
lekkerwater-beach-lodge-at-de-hoop

— 15 —
THE OYSTER BOX

SOUTH AFRICA

Umhlanga Rocks
Durban, KwaZulu-Natal

QUINTESSENTIAL
AFRICAN SEASIDE

◆ TO VISIT BEFORE YOU DIE BECAUSE
This is the ultimate lounge-by-the-pool holiday in true vintage style.

This landmark hotel looks out over the Indian Ocean and the historic lighthouse, which towers just in front of the 80 classic and beautifully decorated rooms and suites. There's a serious whiff of colonial charm about the setting with opulently decorated restaurants and bars, where G&Ts are served in old-fashioned style. The Oyster Box is one of the most beautiful beachside hotels in South Africa and probably the most iconic spot to grab a plate of impossibly fresh oysters with a glass of crisp South African Sauvignon Blanc.

€€
From €310 / US$350 per night in B&B.

www.oysterboxhotel.com

STERREKOPJE HEALING FARM

SOUTH AFRICA | **The Winelands**
Franschhoek | A PLACE FOR HEALING

◆ TO VISIT BEFORE YOU DIE BECAUSE

This retreat is all about the new rural chic in South Africa's stunning Winelands.

After staying at Sterrekopje Healing Farm, most guests want to keep this retreat a well-kept secret. Fans of rural chic claim this is the hottest, most beautiful farm stay – and refuge for the soul – with a big focus on rejuvenation and relaxation. Dotted around the farm's 50 hectares of wilderness are 11 unique sanctuaries and suites, each with an incredible, beautifully warm and rich design of hand-crafted items and voluptuous fabrics and colours. Every day, the adjacent farm building produces the most wonderful organic products and the food is packed with wild flavours. The farm often organises themed stays, from a 'wise woman retreat' to family specials to (re)connect with the little ones. The most beautiful part of the old farm – dating back to 1694 – is the kitchen where guests gather to eat, drink, meet or just relax by the open fire.

€€€
From €750 / US$807 per person per night, all inclusive.

ANDBEYOND GRUMETI
SERENGETI RIVER LODGE

TANZANIA

Western Serengeti
Grumeti River

AFRICAN
CHIC

◆ TO VISIT BEFORE YOU DIE BECAUSE
This sleek safari lodge is one of the most gorgeous in this prime location.

Placed on the banks of a tributary of the Grumeti River in Tanzania's secluded Western Serengeti, &Beyond Grumeti Serengeti River Lodge offers the most beautiful mix of design with the perfect safari experience. Inspired by traditional Maasai manyattas (circular enclosures), the lodge unfolds in a luxurious embrace of the natural world. There are just ten spacious guest suites, each with a private plunge pool and stellar views over the wilderness. Go on a legendary game drive in customised Land Rovers to see the awe-inspiring Great Migration, where millions of wildebeest and zebra thunder across the plains. Tired of bobbing around in 4x4s? Just stay in the lodge and observe the resident pod of hippos lounging in the river. More relaxation awaits at the 25-metre-long basalt stone pool, or in the onsite spa. At night there are those fabulous African skies to marvel at while sipping G&Ts next to an open fire.

€€€
From €1,500 / US$1,634 per night for a double room on all inclusive.

www.andbeyond.com/our-lodges/africa/tanzania/serengeti-national-park/
andbeyond-grumeti-serengeti-river-lodge

— 18 —
BUMI HILLS SAFARI LODGE

ZIMBABWE

Matusadona National Park
Lake Kariba

**ICONIC LAKESIDE
SAFARI LOCATION**

◆ TO VISIT BEFORE YOU DIE BECAUSE

You can take in the 360-degree views over one of the most breathtaking lakes in the world.

For Zimbabweans, the Bumi Hills Safari Lodge is as iconic as the magnificent Lake Kariba it overlooks. The lodge, the oldest and most renowned resort on the shores of the lake, was recently acquired, refurbished and reopened under the African Bush Camps banner. Its new style, look and design are chic and contemporary and the spectacular views and surroundings are just as surreal as ever. Every room looks out onto the lake and the bush below, where wild animals roam freely. There's a spa, an amazing swimming pool with lots of loungers, and in the evening the kitchen team organizes a typical braai (BBQ), which you enjoy beneath a canopy of twinkling candles with the sound of wild Africa in the distance.

€€
From €440 / US$495 per person per night, all inclusive.

— 19 —
VICTORIA FALLS HOTEL

| ZIMBABWE | **Matabeleland** | MAJESTIC |
| | Victoria Falls | GRANDE DAME |

◆ TO VISIT BEFORE YOU DIE BECAUSE

This is one of Southern Africa's true colonial gems.

According to most Zimbabweans, the famed Victoria Falls should be visited from their side and not from Zambia. A must-do is staying at the Victoria Falls Hotel, the epitome of colonial nostalgia. The hotel has recently been refurbished, which means you can now stay in stylish rooms, yet still inhale the charming colonial atmosphere. Another reason to stay here is the terrace with stunning views over Victoria Falls Bridge and the falls, whose local name is Mosi-oa-Tunya, meaning 'smoke that thunders'.

There is no better spot in Africa to order a classic G&T in Stanley's Bar and enjoy the colonial setting of this pure gem.

€€
From €420 / US$470 per night.

— 20 —
WHITE DESERT

ANTARCTICA	**Norwegian territory** Queen Maud Land	**ONLY FOR THE ADVENTUROUS HAPPY FEW**

◆ TO VISIT BEFORE YOU DIE BECAUSE

This is the ultimate and unparalleled end-of-the-world escape.

Prepare to be wowed (and to pay for it!) at this one-of-a-kind 'hotel', where luxury reaches new extremes through a blend of unconventional comfort and adventure. Even reaching White Desert, located on mainland Antarctica, is special: the only way to get there is by taking a 5-hour flight from Cape Town, South Africa between November and February. White Desert isn't a single camp, but a company offering luxurious glamping experiences in Antarctica's remote interior. Whichaway Camp, known for its six cosy 'polar pods' on the ice-free shores of a frozen freshwater lake, and the futuristic Echo Camp, with its space-age 'sky pods',

can each accommodate a maximum of 12 guests. Wolf's Fang sits in Queen Maud Land and, despite its remote location, boasts ensuite tents, a shared lounge, and a cosy dining area for meeting like-minded travellers. Take an extra flight to witness awe-inspiring emperor penguins and their fluffy chicks, or for the ultimate explorer, pay a visit to the Geographic South Pole. Each camp vanishes without a trace each season, leaving the environment untouched and ready for another harsh and extreme polar winter.

€€€€
From €65,000 / US$69,949 per person,
with flights from Cape Town to Antarctica included.

https://white-desert.com

— 21 —
GRAN HOTEL MANZANA KEMPINSKI LA HABANA

CARIBBEAN

Cuba
Havana

RESTORATION
OF LOST GLORY

◆ TO VISIT BEFORE YOU DIE BECAUSE

Beautiful and mesmerizing Havana deserves a true luxury hotel like this.

This iconic institution is the first ever luxury hotel in Havana. Perfectly located in the heart of Old Havana, the hotel has 246 rooms and suites, all decorated in a modern colonial style, with high ceilings and French windows and shutters opening up onto the vibrant historic town. Smoke a cigar in the hotel's Evocación tobacco lounge while sipping from a selection of fine rums, or enjoy a swim in Havana's first rooftop pool. Outside the hotel there's Ernest Hemingway's old drinking hole, Floridita, and the entrance to Calle Obispo – the gateway to cafés, restaurants and key sights.

€€
From €240 / US$270 per night for a double room, with breakfast.

48

www.kempinski.com/en/havana/gran-hotel-kempinski-la-habana

GOLDENEYE

CARIBBEAN   Jamaica   JAMES BOND
                  North Coast   OUTPOST

◆ TO VISIT BEFORE YOU DIE BECAUSE

This iconic writer's retreat is located on one of the most colourful islands in the world.

Ian Fleming, author of the James Bond novels, bought this original clifftop piece of land in 1946 and built a simple house within a sunken garden with views over the ocean. Today, this is the flagship Fleming Villa, consisting of a comfortable three-bedroom hideaway and two one-bedroom cottages, a pool and private beach. GoldenEye is a hip, luxurious resort built around the villa where Fleming wrote 14 James Bond novels. There is a blue lagoon, lots of beaches and several accommodation options from villas to more simple beach huts. Enjoy a grilled octopus at The Gazebo, a treehouse-style restaurant, open for drinks and dinner.

€€
From €320 / US$360 per night for a double room, with breakfast.

| CARIBBEAN | **Saint Lucia**
Soufrière | TROPICAL
MODERNISM |

◆ TO VISIT BEFORE YOU DIE BECAUSE

This is the absolute number-one resort in the region for lovers of romance and fascinating architecture.

Lovers of dreamy, island-style resorts call Jade Mountain the most striking and iconic hotel in the Caribbean. It's a bold-looking place with probably one of the best views of the wide ocean and the Pitons, the iconic mountains of Saint Lucia. It's no surprise this is a favourite honeymoon destination, where couples hide away in one of the 29 gorgeous suites with open-plan living room and views over the Pitons from the infinity pool or whirlpool tub. More romance is found at the Jade Mountain Club with more striking vistas and dishes made from produce from the Anse Chastanet estate and its nearby organic farm.

€€€€
From €2,000 / US$2,245 per night, all inclusive.

www.jademountainstlucia.com

| CANADA | Fogo Island | REMOTE |
| | Newfoundland | REVIVAL |

◆ TO VISIT BEFORE YOU DIE BECAUSE

This is the most fairy-tale-like hotel in Canada, located in a far-flung corner of the world.

The journey to tiny Fogo Island with its charismatic Fogo Island Inn is a true adventure, especially in winter, when the Atlantic Ocean freezes around the north coast of Newfoundland and Arctic storms sweep across the land. All the suites have floor-to-ceiling windows with a view over the Labrador Sea. In spring, gigantic icebergs float by, tracing the quiet coastline. There is no doubt you will feel remote here: according to the Flat Earth Society, Brimstone Head on Fogo Island is one of the four corners of the earth.

€€€
From €550 / US$620 per night for a double room, full board.

CANADA	**Vancouver Island** Broughton Archipelago	WILDERNESS OUTPOST

◆ TO VISIT BEFORE YOU DIE BECAUSE
This is a life-changing dive deep into the fjord-like wilderness of Vancouver Island.

When Craig and Deborah Murray, the parents of the current owner, Fraser Murray, bought an old floating house in the pristine Broughton Archipelago in 1980 to escape their busy lives, they wanted to create one of the wildest places to stay in North America. Nimmo Bay Wilderness, a former fisherman lodge, has been transformed into a luxurious refuge where easy adventures such as hiking, kayaking, fishing, heli trips, paddle boarding and boat jaunts show guests the real heart of this remote territory. The Murray family has recently built a collection of new wooden stilt houses in which luxurious rooms are hidden. In the old, floating saloon where guests meet, there's always hearty, home-made food or a local seafood feast on offer. A real treat after a day out in the wild.

€€€€
From €1,000 / US$1,120 per person per night, all inclusive.

THE WICKANINNISH INN

CANADA

Vancouver Island
Tofino

STORM
GAZING

◆ TO VISIT BEFORE YOU DIE BECAUSE

There is no better place to watch storms roll in from the Pacific than from your hotel room window.

It's invigorating to stay at the edge of the Pacific Ocean on the wild west coast of Vancouver Island, but not just in any hotel. In this perfectly positioned beachfront hotel, every room gazes out over the magnificent Pacific and the sandy beach of Tofino, where surfers gather and beach lovers go for long coastal walks to spot whales and soaring eagles. All rooms have a fireplace and a soaking tub with more views over the ocean. Downstairs, The Pointe, with floor-to-ceiling panoramic views of the ocean, serves brunch, lunch and dinner, and the Driftwood Café in the hotel's Beach Building is open for breakfast, lunch and light dinner.

€€
From €210 / US$235 per night for a double room, with breakfast.

www.wickinn.com

MEXICO	Yucatán	ISLAND
	Holbox	GETAWAY

TO VISIT BEFORE YOU DIE BECAUSE

A relaxed Mexican island with an intimate luxury hotel is the perfect holiday combo.

Holbox Island, just off the coast from Cancún, is still one of Mexico's best-kept secrets. The car-free island is boho-chic with cobalt-blue water and brilliant white beaches, and Ser Casasandra is the perfect remote retreat. The hotel is hidden under a thatched roof, elegantly draped over the first floor where, along the balcony, white cotton curtains stir gently in the warm air. The private beach in front of the hotel tempts you with private lounge beds and a bar that serves cool drinks and light lunch dishes. In the back garden there's a small tear-shaped swimming pool with sun loungers and beds. Ser Casasandra has 20 suites arranged in two free-standing buildings in the garden, while other suites, some of which have ocean views from their terraces, are located on the top floor of the main building.

€€
From €240 / US$270 per night for a double room, with breakfast.

www.casasandra.com

MEXICO	Mexico City	URBAN
	Polanco	REFUGE

◆ TO VISIT BEFORE YOU DIE BECAUSE

This is the new darling of Mexico City's most ritzy and lively neighbourhood.

This is no ordinary city hotel: Casa Polanco is housed in a meticulously restored private residence dating from the 1940s, where classic Spanish colonial revival architecture rubs shoulders with modern design elements. The hotel is intimate with only 19 stunning rooms and suites, each with a private balcony overlooking the hotel's lush gardens. Some rooms have gorgeous crown moulding and they all have stunning art and decorative pieces by Mexican creatives like Ricardo Mazal, Jordi Boldó and Graciela Iturbide. Every room comes with a complimentary minibar stocked with treats like matcha-covered blueberries as well as bath-and-body products developed in partnership with Xinú, a chic perfumery from the neighbourhood. The hotel also has a pleasant terrace next to La Veranda restaurant serving light and local dishes.

€€€
From €450 / US$490 for a double room with breakfast.

www.casapolanco.com

61

150 HOTELS YOU NEED TO VISIT BEFORE YOU DIE

USA	Utah	DESERT
	Lake Powell	DREAMS

◆ TO VISIT BEFORE YOU DIE BECAUSE

This is the most stunning, subtly designed hotel in the USA with ultimate desert vistas.

The clever design of Amangiri is inspired by the rugged nature of the Utah landscape and the distinctive Entrada Sandstone. Guests come here to relax around the swimming pool that curves around a rock formation, or to recharge in the 2,300-square-metre (25,000-square-foot) Aman Spa with sweeping desert views and unique Navajo-inspired treatments. All 34 rooms and suites extend from the main building into the desert, almost like an eagle's wing. Every room has a view of the untamed landscape , and the panoramic vistas can also be enjoyed from the bath or the bed. The large folding windows can be completely opened onto the private terrace with a fire pit, the perfect place to marvel at the starry skies in the intensely black nights of southern Utah. Located a five-minute drive from the resort, Amangiri has recently opened Camp Sarika, which has ten brand-new, luxurious tented pavilions.

€€€€
From €1,550 / US$1,740 per night for a double room, minibar included.

https://www.aman.com/resorts/amangiri

— 30 —
THE LUDLOW

USA

New York City
Lower East Side

COOL CAT
ELEGANCE

◆ TO VISIT BEFORE YOU DIE BECAUSE

There is no other NYC boutique hotel where you instantly feel part of the stylish, relaxed hood.

Ludlow Street, in the heart of the Lower East Side, is well known for its thriving art and music scene. The street boasts an abundance of bars and eateries with curbside terraces, and just around the corner is the famous Katz Deli (where the famous Meg Ryan scene in *When Harry Met Sally...* was filmed). When sitting in The Ludlow lobby and bar downstairs, with its dark and cosy interior, open fireplaces and courtyard patio, it's hard to imagine that the hotel has 175 rooms and suites. The style is imbued with NYC elegance with two-poster beds, comfy armchairs, marble tables and amazing views over the skyline of the city from some of the rooms. Another attraction is the hotel restaurant, Dirty French, the NYC version of a French bistro and hugely popular with locals.

€€
From €170 / US$190 per night for a double room.

www.ludlowhotel.com

— 31 —
ULTIMA THULE
LODGE

USA

Alaska
Wrangell-St. Elias National Park and Preserve

WILD
FRONTIER

◆ TO VISIT BEFORE YOU DIE BECAUSE

This is a journey into the extreme wild corners of Alaska but with the bonus of staying in a comfortable remote lodge.

Welcome to the deep Alaskan wilderness, accessible only by bush plane. Ultima Thule Lodge is located some 150 kilometres (90 miles) from civilization, in the Wrangell-St. Elias National Park and Preserve, one of the largest areas of protected landscape on the planet. No roads, no cars and almost no people, but plenty of black and brown bears. Owner and aviator Paul Claus and his family are highly skilled bush pilots who will prepare you a festive, home-cooked dinner of roast salmon in the comfort and warmth of their huge log house and then take you out in their Super Cub, Alpha, to land on glaciers or go white-water rafting down the Chitina River.

€€€€
From €7,700 / US$8,640 per person for a 4-night all inclusive package, with small plane transfers.

HOUSE
OF JASMINES

ARGENTINA

Salta
Salta City

ESTANCIA
DREAMS

◆ TO VISIT BEFORE YOU DIE BECAUSE

The dreamy, wild region of Salta is the perfect backdrop for this gem of a boutique hotel.

American movie star Robert Duvall and his Argentine wife, Luciana, turned this 120-year-old eccentric ranch house, set in expansive orchards and gardens of roses and jasmine, into a gorgeous boutique hotel. The current owners, Raoul and Stéphanie Fenestraz, run it with as much passion and love for their country and region. The small hotel, located just outside the colonial city of Salta in the tall shadow of the Andes, has seven elegantly decorated guest rooms, some with a private terrace overlooking the gardens, fields and mountains beyond. The restaurant serves farm to table dishes and local wine on the wonderful terrace with a view of the Andes.

€
From €140 / US$160 per night for a double room, with breakfast.

www.houseofjasmines.com

ESTANCIA RINCÓN CHICO

ARGENTINA

Patagonia
Valdes Peninsula

PATAGONIAN ESCAPE

◆ TO VISIT BEFORE YOU DIE BECAUSE

To live the true, Patagonian estancia lifestyle close the Atlantic Ocean is an unforgettable experience.

Located on the popular Valdes Peninsula, Rincón Chico is still a working estancia with merino sheep and also serves as a scientific base for wildlife research. The estancia is typically Patagonian in style, with corrugated metal roofs and old wooden floors with lots of burning fires inside for when the cold Patagonian winds that blow in from the Atlantic Ocean pick up. The estancia has eight modest but comfortable rooms, all looking out over the vast grassland, and opening onto a shared veranda. All meals are included, with the focus on hearty home-cooked food based on family recipes such as lamb asado and pungent stews, perfect after a day of whale and penguin watching.

€€€
From €750 / US$840 per night for a double room, full board.

www.rinconchico.com.ar

— 34 —
PALACIO
DUHAU PARK HYATT

ARGENTINA	Buenos Aires	URBAN
	Recoleta	PALACE

◆ TO VISIT BEFORE YOU DIE BECAUSE

In a city filled with excitement and buzz, a tranquil classic bolt-hole like this is all you need.

This is by far the most iconic hotel in Buenos Aires: grand, uber-stylish, glitzy and glamourous. The old palace has been perfectly renovated with stunning suites and rooms and a tranquil, lush garden connecting the old building to a new-style wing with more luxurious rooms, some with a balcony, giving way to buzzy Recoleta. Equally charming are the three restaurants and candlelit patios and gardens where you can listen to birdsongs and peacefully drink and dine, away from busy Buenos Aires. The breakfast is the loveliest in the city and the cheese selection, locally made in Argentina, is amazing with the elaborate wine bar offer.

€€
From €250 / US$280 per night for a double room.

www.hyatt.com/en-US/hotel/argentina/
palacio-duhau-park-hyatt-buenos-aires/bueph

— 35 —
COPACABANA PALACE

BRAZIL

Rio de Janeiro
Copacabana Beach

LEGENDARY LOCATION

◆ TO VISIT BEFORE YOU DIE BECAUSE

There is no other hotel that looks out onto one of the most iconic beach settings in the world.

The Palace has looked out over Copacabana for almost a century. While the world-famous beach is lively and often wild, the hotel is gracefully neoclassical in style with endless slabs of marble and dark wood. The 147 rooms are in the same classic style, and those with views over the ocean are the best. The hotel has a one-star Michelin restaurant. The main attraction, however, is the poolside Pérgula for a leisurely Sunday lunch (all you can eat and drink) or a relaxing cocktail as the sun sets. For those wanting to exercise, there's a rooftop tennis court with views over the beach.

€€
From €240 / US$270 per night for a double room, with breakfast.

www.belmond.com/hotels/south-america/brazil/
rio-de-janeiro/belmond-copacabana-palace

150 HOTELS YOU NEED TO VISIT BEFORE YOU DIE

— 36 —
BARRACUDA
HOTEL & VILLAS

BRAZIL

Bahia

Itacaré

SWEDISH
EXOTICISM

◆ TO VISIT BEFORE YOU DIE BECAUSE

This is the perfect cocktail of tropical Bahia
and Scandi-style aesthetics.

The Barracuda is an original *pousada* (inn)-style concept developed by a group of friends, Swedish entrepreneurs and a Brazilian couple, who in 2005 created their own paradise alongside a tropical beach in Itacaré, a few hours south of Salvador. The Barracuda is the perfect spot to surf and dive deep into the Bahia beach vibe, with 26 suites and 12 private villas overlooking the Atlantic. Get more tropical vibes at the Beach Cabana that serves seafood and cocktails after a long afternoon of surfing.

€€
From €370 / US$415 per night with breakfast.

www.thebarracuda.com.br

73

— 37 —
EXPLORA RAPA NUI

CHILE

Territory of Chile
Easter Island

MAGICAL
VIBES

◆ TO VISIT BEFORE YOU DIE BECAUSE

Travelling to this island and bedding down here is imbued with a magical, strong sense of place.

Rapa Nui, aka Easter Island, is the most remote inhabited island in the world. It has an airfield, and a flight from either South America or Tahiti takes about five-and-a-half-hours. The isolated location of the island is pretty magical, but Rapa Nui has another kind of magic. Almost every stone, every location, every detail has symbolic meaning. In a remote location away from town, you can bed down at Explora Rapa Nui, which looks out over the green landscape of the island and the sea. Chilean architect José Cruz

Ovalle has won several awards for the clever, sleek design of the hotel, which so perfectly blends into its surroundings that it seems to disappear. The low buildings are entirely constructed from local materials and the huge windows in every room afford fine views of the island with the occasional wild horse peeking in.

€€€
From €480 / US$540 per person per night, all inclusive.

www.explora.com/easter-island-hotels

CHILE	Patagonia	PREMIUM
	Torres del Paine	VIEWS

◆ TO VISIT BEFORE YOU DIE BECAUSE

This is an amazing location near the famous Torres del Paine National Park, far away from the crowds.

Tierra Patagonia offers stunning views over the shores of Lake Sarmiento and the famous Paine Massif, a snow-covered marvel that changes colour as the light and shadows shift throughout the day. It's blissfully quiet here in the vast Chilean Patagonia, and the national park is just a 15-minute drive away. The architecture blends into the landscape, featuring a curved wooden structure with huge windows looking out over the landscape. The bar and restaurant are in one airy, open space and serve hearty, pleasant dishes to warm you up after a day out. There's also a lovely intimate library with sheep skins and comfy sofas.

€€€
From €1,800 / US$2,020 per person for three nights, all inclusive.

ANDBEYOND VIRA VIRA

CHILE

Lake District
Pucón

NATURAL LUXURY

◆ TO VISIT BEFORE YOU DIE BECAUSE

Being surrounded by snow-capped volcanoes while bathing in luxury should be on every bucket list.

This modern, luxury-style hacienda boutique hotel is only a short distance away from the beautiful Lake Villarrica and town of Pucón, surrounded by snow-peaked volcanoes and next to the fast-flowing Liucura River. Although the hotel is modern in style, its exterior and interior flow over into the natural landscape with lots of subtle colours and fabrics and contemporary artefacts from the local Mapuche culture. There are six suites in the main building and 12 villas

with high ceilings and windows just next to the river, where horses roam freely. Vira Vira is the perfect place to enjoy a glass of Chilean wine with a three-course lunch. Sit outside on the patio next to a large pond and tuck into home-grown salads and greens served with local salmon or lamb.

€€€
From €650 / US$730 per person per night, all inclusive, with some activities and (alcoholic) drinks included.

www.andbeyond.com/our-lodges/south-america/
chile/lake-district/andbeyond-vira-vira

URUGUAY

Maldonado
Pueblo de Garzón

PUEBLO
CHARM

◆ TO VISIT BEFORE YOU DIE BECAUSE

This tiny village resembles the setting of a dusty cowboy movie with the hotel as its little piece of heaven.

Garzón Hotel and Restaurant is a pretty little gem where you experience the true nature of the Uruguayan countryside. Next to the wonderful restaurant are five suites located in a large brick house that was once the village's general store. All the rooms look out onto the garden and swimming pool and have a fireplace or wood burner. This is the perfect culinary haven if you want to eat the best local food and drink fine local wines without having to leave the retreat.

€€
From €240 / US$270 per night in a double room with breakfast.

POSADA AYANA

URUGUAY	**Maldonado**	ARTFUL
	José Ignacio	EXPERIENCE

◆ TO VISIT BEFORE YOU DIE BECAUSE

This might be South America's cutest oceanside boutique hotel.

Hidden away in José Ignacio, a charming Uruguayan fishing village near Punta del Este, Posada Ayana is a stunningly restored 200-year-old farmhouse. Think classic Spanish colonial architecture with modern touches, celebrating local heritage in a refreshingly contemporary way. There are only 18 stunning rooms and suites (plus a private villa for up to six people), all with private balconies overlooking the lush gardens or ocean, creating a connection with nature. Another reason to stay here is the Skyspace Ta Khut, the first free-standing work of its kind in South America by renowned light artist James Turrell. This mesmerising installation resembles a white marble stupa, offering an immersive experience focused on the sky. Inside, a blue marble relief of the Milky Way's centre aligns with the actual night sky, creating a breathtaking connection between art and nature. As well as world-class art there is stellar farm-to-table cuisine featuring seasonal, locally sourced ingredients from both the ocean and land.

€€
From €400 / US$435 for a double room
with breakfast.

www.posada-ayana.com

— 42 —
GANGTEY LODGE

BHUTAN

Phobjikha Valley
Gangtey

HIMALAYAN
REFUGE

◆ TO VISIT BEFORE YOU DIE BECAUSE
This is the only privately owned boutique hotel in the country.

Gantey Lodge is an intimate collection of 12 rooms looking out over the magical Phobjikha Valley with beautiful communal spaces that blend into the dreamlike setting in the distance. The lodge is a stunning example of Bhutanese architecture and includes rustic details such as earthy tones, local stones and wooden artefacts . The elegant decor gives the lodge a warm homely feeling, even in the bedrooms, especially in winter when all the fireplaces are lit. One of the highlights after a day of exploring the valley is a steaming-hot bath with wide views over the dense forest and the dreamlike monastery in the distance.

€€€
From €440 / US$495 per night, full board.

— 43 —
AMANSARA

CAMBODIA

Siem Reap
French Quarter

ROYAL
VILLA

◆ TO VISIT BEFORE YOU DIE BECAUSE
This is a wonderfully private hotel in Cambodia, wrapped in stunning
New Khmer-style architecture.

Jackie Kennedy, Charles de Gaulle and Angelina Jolie are a few of the distinguished guests who have come to hide away in this former New Khmer-style villa located in the Old French Quarter of Siem Reap. The style is modernist vintage, and the hotel's airy coolness is perfect after a day out in steamy Siem Reap visiting Angkor Wat and its surroundings. The old villa has been lovingly renovated with 12 pool-side suites set around a private green courtyard and the stunning pool. The dining room is the former ballroom whose circular ceiling givess the place a very unique ambiance. The menu includes both Cambodian and Western dishes. A fun detail is that guests are picked up and dropped off at the airport in one of King Sihanouk's old 1960s Mercedes.

€€€
From €1,250 / US$1,400 per night for a double room, with breakfast and dinner.

www.aman.com/resorts/amansara

— 44 —
KNAI BANG
CHATT

CAMBODIA	Krong Kaeb	VILLA
	Kep	STYLE

◆ TO VISIT BEFORE YOU DIE BECAUSE
The Khmer-style modernistic beachside vibes are matchless.

It's only a two-hour drive from hectic Phnom Penh to the most inspiring beachside retreat in Cambodia. The Belgian-owned Knai Bang Chatt is a hidden gem with unparalleled views over the Gulf of Thailand. The hotel is an old Khmer villa in true modernist style, carefully renovated and restyled into a haven of tranquillity. There are no TVs in the rooms, giving you the peace to enjoy the killer views over the water to the chic Sailing Club Restaurant and Bar, as surfers and sailing boats glide by. At the restaurant smart dishes and cocktails are served while guests dine almost *les pieds dans l'eau*.

€
From €105 / US$120 per night, breakfast included.

www.knaibangchatt.com

— 45 —
BANYAN TREE RINGHA

CHINA

Shangri-La
Jiangtang

TIBETAN
TREASURE

◆ TO VISIT BEFORE YOU DIE BECAUSE

Nowhere else will you find stellar architecture and private access to the Great Wall of China.

Set in the heart of Shangri-La (formerly Zhongdian County) and far away from China's hectic cities, Banyan Tree Ringha has the appeal of a Tibetan village with all the modern commodities of an urban hotel to make your stay in this quiet corner simply perfect. The 32 suites and lodges are all hidden in old and restored farmhouse-style dwellings. The rooms are little treasures with soft lighting, dark woods and gorgeous lacquered furniture.

Rural paths lead from the rooms to a central area with a spa, a lobby lounge offering Chinese teas, and two restaurants: Llamo, serving Tibetan and Western cuisine, and Chang-Sa, offering drinks and Tibetan hotpots, a must-try specialty from this region.

€
From €130 / US$145 per night for a double room, with breakfast.

GRAND HYATT HONG KONG

HONG KONG

Central
Wan Chai Waterfront

BIG AND BRIGHT

◆ TO VISIT BEFORE YOU DIE BECAUSE

You can enjoy Hong Kong in true luxury and style without breaking the bank.

Even though small boutique hotels are the current trend, there is nothing wrong with choosing a large (chain) hotel to bed down in a frantic city in true style. A good example of how 'grand' (and affordable) a large hotel can be is the wonderful Grand Hyatt next to the waterfront in Central Hong Kong and a short walk away from the Wan Chai Star Ferry Pier. The lobby is lavish with black marble and gold-leaf decor, as well as swirling staircases leading to upper floors with amazing restaurants and bars. The best rooms are those with harbour views and Club Lounge access where long breakfasts, cocktail hours and immaculate service is included. The decor of the rooms is clean and neutral with light colours and Asian-themed art.

€
From €140 / US$160 per night for a double room, with breakfast.

www.hyatt.com/en-US/hotel/china/grand-hyatt-hong-kong/hkggh

MANDARIN ORIENTAL
HONG KONG

HONG KONG	Central	LUXURY
	Connaught Road	LANDMARK

◆ TO VISIT BEFORE YOU DIE BECAUSE

This hotel is the epitome of Hong Kong, a mix of Asia and the West in a truly exceptional style.

The Mandarin Oriental is by far the most iconic hotel in the city. Surrounded by some of Hong Kong's most eye-catching and historic buildings, it has been attracting a loyal and famous clientele since 1963. The hotel's service is immaculate, and there's a special buzz that creates a perfect mix for both leisure and business travellers. The hotel's 499 rooms are ultra-comfortable with a decor of soft colours and gold and lacquered woods. The best rooms offer views of Statue Square and Victoria Harbour with the ever-changing light over the water. The top-rated breakfast includes a large variety of options from prawn dumplings to the perfectly cooked eggs Benedict. Upstairs there's the Man Wah, serving classic Cantonese dishes, and Pierre, featuring the French cuisine of three-Michelin-starred chef Pierre Gagnaire.

€€
From €230 / US$260 per night for a double room, with breakfast.

— 48 —
AMANBAGH

INDIA	Rajasthan Bhangarh	ENCHANTED VALLEY

◆ TO VISIT BEFORE YOU DIE BECAUSE
Surrounding this luxurious hidden treasure are the ruins of an ancient empire.

The enchanted rural hamlet of Bhangarh, located about 300 kilometres (185 miles) from Delhi in the Alwar district of Rajasthan, is often overlooked by travellers. The Alwar district has fertile valleys where clean streams flow, mango and date trees grow, and the scent of eucalyptus lingers in the air. Amanbagh is no ordinary hotel, but rather a cluster of soft-pink sandstone buildings with 40 suites, clean and minimalist, with lots of polished stones and wood, set in a lush garden of exotic plants and trees. The hotel has one of the most stunning pools in India, which can be marvelled at from colonnaded terraces where you can enjoy a relaxed Indian-style breakfast or an uber-romantic dinner surrounded by thousands of flickering candles.

€€€
From €650 / US$730 per night in a double room, with breakfast.

www.aman.com/resorts/amanbagh

— 49 —
TAJ LAKE PALACE

Udaipur
Lake Pichola

◆ TO VISIT BEFORE YOU DIE BECAUSE

The views from the dreamlike setting of this historic landmark are out of this world.

Imagine staying at a 272-year-old white marble palace, floating like an illusion in the centre of the tranquil and glassy Lake Pichola in enigmatic Rajasthan. Ask any India expert and they will tell you that the Taj Lake Palace is India's most romantic hotel. Built by a prince as a summer retreat, the hotel is now a beacon of luxury with 65 rooms and 18 grand suites, all with magnificent views of the neighbouring City Palace, the Machla Magra and the Aravalli Hills. Go for fine dining at Bhairo, a breathtaking rooftop restaurant with sparkling views of the beautifully lit palace and the glistening waters of dreamy Lake Pichola.

€€
From €220 / US$250 per night for a double room, with breakfast.

CHAMBA CAMP
THIKSEY

INDIA

Ladakh
Manali Road, Thiksey

CHIC CAMPING

◆ TO VISIT BEFORE YOU DIE BECAUSE

**You will wake up with views over the Himalayas and the sound of
the Shankha (conch shell) from the nearby gompa.**

There's something extraordinary about flying from bustling Delhi to remote Leh, the capital of Ladakh in India. This pleasant bubble of human settlement, located in the endlessly stretching Himalayas, at an altitude of 3,500 metres (11,500 feet), is one of the highest cities in the world. The most beautiful place to bed down is the luxurious Chamba Camp near the Thiksey Monastery, one of the most important religious sites in the vicinity of Leh. The divinely furnished tents radiate an old-world charm reminiscent of the Raj, combined with outstanding luxury – all the tents come equipped with creature comforts you would expect to find in a luxury hotel room. In the distance rises the gorgeous Thiksey Monastery painted in the natural reddish and chalky-white colours so typical of this mountainous region.

€€€
From €900 / US$1,010 per night in a tent
for two people in full board.

https://tutc.com/chamba-camp-thiksey.php

— 51 —
RAAS DEVIGARH

INDIA

Rajasthan
Delwara

FORT
FANTASY

◆ TO VISIT BEFORE YOU DIE BECAUSE

While many fort hotels in India are dark and gloomy, this is the brightest and nicest of them all.

Set in dreamy, landscaped gardens, this gorgeous fort hotel was rebuilt to its former glory, with the rather modern, minimalist look and feel of its interior design contrasting starkly with the historic architecture of its facades. Raas Devigarh hides 39 stunning suites throughout the fort, all with pale marble floors and private outdoor spaces. Dig into proper Rajasthani curries and a spicy breakfast that includes glorious masala dosa. And there's also hearty Western fare with greens from the hotel's organic garden.

€
From €110 / US$125 per night for a double room, with breakfast.

— 52 —
NIHI SUMBA

INDONESIA	Sumba Island	HIDDEN
	Nihiwatu	HAVEN

◆ TO VISIT BEFORE YOU DIE BECAUSE

The cliché of barefoot luxury is taken to the next level in this Indonesian tropical paradise.

It takes some effort to get here: an hour's flight from Bali to Sumba Island where tourism is almost non-existent and nature and traditions are still key. Located along a forested border of long golden beach, the Nihi Sumba resort was originally all about surfing, until it was transformed into one of the most luxurious retreats in Asia. The elegant villas have the pointy thatched roofs so typical of Sumba, and they all come with private infinity pools set in gardens of banana and frangipani trees. You can still surf, but you can also ride a pony into the ocean, try paddle boarding, or just dive under water to explore another world.

€€
From €450 / US$505 per night for a double room, with breakfast and dinner.

INDONESIA	Bali	JUNGLE
	Ubud	JOY

◆ TO VISIT BEFORE YOU DIE BECAUSE

This hotel mixes the beauty and charm of Bali with true Japanese hospitality.

There are many stunning places dotting the lush Ubud jungle in Bali, but Hoshinoya Bali is unlike any other. Owned by a top Japanese hotel brand, it's the only retreat embracing *omotenashi* (exceptional hospitality) while immersing guests in the charm of Ubud's incredible emerald forest. Imagine 30 free-standing villas, each a haven of privacy with a private infinity pool overlooking the misty, crisp jungle canopy. The design is sleek yet sustainable, using locally sourced bamboo and volcanic rock. Rooftop gardens provide fresh ingredients for the on-site restaurant and cafe, two beautiful spots for experiencing the incredible food of Bali. Dive into Balinese culture with a guided rice paddy trek, join a traditional cooking class, or just relax in the spa inspired by ancient Indonesian wellness practices.

€€
From €240 / US$261 per room, per night.

WASURE NO SATO GAJOEN

JAPAN	**Kyushu** Myoken Onsen	TUCKED-AWAY SERENITY

◆ TO VISIT BEFORE YOU DIE BECAUSE

Here you plunge into the essence of Japanese hot-spring culture.

Wasure no sato Gajoen is hidden away in the sleepy hot-spring town of Myoken Onsen, next to the fast-flowing Amorigawa River, where hens roam freely and nature is intense. The ryokan-style rooms have exposed dark wooden beams, tatami flooring and futon-style bedding; no Western style to be found here. The best rooms have private open-air hot-spring baths with wide wooden terraces. The three daily meals are all about home-grown, organic ingredients, and the meat and the vegetables come from the hotel's farm and garden.

€€€
From €570 / US$640 per night for a double room, with breakfast and dinner.

HOSHINOYA
KARUIZAWA

JAPAN	**Nagano** Karuizawa	HOT SPRING HAPPINESS

◆ TO VISIT BEFORE YOU DIE BECAUSE

This is the new style of hot springs where modern meets Japanese tradition in harmony.

Take the bullet train from Tokyo Station, and in just over an hour the view of the Yukawa River means that you've reached the Hoshinoya Karuizawa Resort. The hotel has 77 stunning villas scattered around a serene garden of running streams and stone paths. For centuries, locals have travelled to Karuizawa to benefit from the healing hot springs and mineral water. The most popular treatment is the Ginjo Sojourn in the huge hot-spring baths, a therapy that uses sake lees (rich in adenosine, great for ageing skin) and *yoh*, an oil made with seasonal herbs. The food served in the main restaurant is modern kaseiki style with different types of sake to try out.

€€€
From €550 / US$620 per night for a double room, half-board.

— 56 —
MANDARIN ORIENTAL TOKYO

JAPAN	**Tokyo** Nihonbashi	HIGH-RISE STYLE

◆ TO VISIT BEFORE YOU DIE BECAUSE

You can grasp the vastness of a city like Tokyo from every subtly sexy room in this hotel.

There are many high-rise hotels in the city, towering above tall office buildings and offering stellar views over the city and Mount Fuji. But the Mandarin Oriental is by far the best on all levels, with its excellent service, stunning rooms with a Tokyo city view, the best breakfast buffet in town, and a handful of amazing bars and restaurants with jaw-dropping panoramas. Popular at the hotel is the small pizza counter in the izakaya-style pizza bar, where Tokyo's best wood-fired oven pizza is served. The 179 rooms are huge for Tokyo and have lots of wood, washi paper and beautiful, traditional details and fabrics with cherry blossom motifs.

€€
From €450 / US$505 per night for a double room, with breakfast.

www.mandarinoriental.com/tokyo/nihonbashi/luxury-hotel

PARK HYATT TOKYO

JAPAN	**Tokyo** West Shinjuku	LOST IN ADMIRATION

◆ TO VISIT BEFORE YOU DIE BECAUSE

This is still a legendary, must-stay hotel, thanks to its starring role in a fabulous Hollywood classic.

This magnificent five-star hotel, located in the Shinjuku district of central Tokyo, rose to fame when it was chosen as a major setting in the 2003 award-winning film *Lost in Translation* starring Bill Murray and Scarlett Johansson. Its fame aside, the Park Hyatt, with its 177 rooms hidden between the 39th and 52nd floor of a classy glass tower, has always been adored for its flawless service, its timeless and elegant design, and its iconic, atmospheric cocktail bar on the top floor with uninterrupted views of Mount Fuji – not to mention the Japanese-style breakfast, which is the best in town (you can have it delivered to your room at no extra charge), and a first-class lap pool and spa.

€€
From €360 / US$405 per night for a double room, with breakfast.

— 58 —
AMANTAKA

LAOS

Luang Prabang
Kingkitsarath Rd

COLONIAL RETREAT

◆ TO VISIT BEFORE YOU DIE BECAUSE
There is Mekong magic in this memorable setting.

Set on a quiet garden estate and housed in graceful 19th-century French buildings in the UNESCO-protected town of Luang Prabang, Amantaka is a true colonial gem. Once a provincial hospital, the hotel, with its 24 rooms – some with a private pool – is luxury redefined. For more privacy there are the standalone Amantaka Suites, encircled by large verandas and private spa treatment quarters. The eye-catcher is the oversized pool in the middle of the sprawling and grassy property where dining on balmy evenings surrounded by countless candles offers an unforgettable experience. Don't forget to cruise along the Mekong River or explore on foot or by bike the chic boutiques and countless eateries in the picturesque town.

€€€
From €920 / US$1,035 for a double room with breakfast.

— 59 —
INLE PRINCESS RESORT

MYANMAR	**Inle Lake** Nyaung Shwe	TRANQUIL SANCTUARY

◆ TO VISIT BEFORE YOU DIE BECAUSE
This lake refuge is by far the dreamiest hotel in Myanmar.

The dynamic Burmese social entrepreneur Yin Myo Su opened the resort in 1998 in a quiet inlet on the eastern shore of the famous Inle Lake as one of the first hotels in the region. Her goal was not only to create a luxurious place to stay and a base to explore the lake, but also to focus on helping the local community, promoting sustainability and protecting the lake environment. The thatched-roof bedrooms are hidden in a lush garden and look out over the reeds and lotus flowers bobbing in the glistening waters. The restaurant serves tasty, traditional Inthar delicacies, and the bar offers local wines and international classics. The most beautiful spot is the huge restaurant terrace, the perfect spot to have breakfast, while the lake slowly wakes up.

€
From €205 / US$230 per night with breakfast.

www.inle-princess.com

PEACOCK GUESTHOUSE

NEPAL	**Kathmandu Valley** Bhaktapur	HIMALAYAN INN

◆ TO VISIT BEFORE YOU DIE BECAUSE

This is time travelling into an intimate Buddhist sanctuary far removed from the world.

The film director Bernardo Bertolucci used this location for the 1993 fictional drama *Little Buddha*. The guesthouse is almost 700 years old and is one of the most ancient inns in the world. There are only nine rooms in this former pilgrims' rest house. The hotel is a little labyrinth with hallways and stairs leading to the simple but charming rooms that include the Baithak room, overlooking the square, and the Veranda rooms with small balconies overlooking the inner courtyard. The food is also simple but entirely locally sourced with a good mix of Nepalese dishes and Western options. At the Himalayan Bakery next door, you can stock up on bread and cakes and even sip a glass of wine.

€
From €45 / US$50 per night for
a double room, with breakfast.

@peacockguesthouse

— 61 —
THE HAPPY HOUSE

NEPAL

The Himalayas
Kaskikot

HIGH-LEVEL
HAPPINESS

◆ TO VISIT BEFORE YOU DIE BECAUSE

This small inn is the perfect example of how a warm, family-run hotel should be.

The Happy House is where Sir Edmund Hillary, the summit-conquering Everest climber, used to stay on his return visits to the Himalayas. Snuggled amidst the terraced hills of Kaskikot, Nepal, this isn't your average hotel. Kaskikot, which was named a 'Model Eco-Village', sits at an altitude of almost 2,500 metres with views over the mighty Dhaulagiri massif, surrounded by pine trees and rhododendron forests, and along an ancient yak-trading route. The village is all about cultural heritage, influenced by both Tibetan and Nepali traditions. Built and run by a welcoming Sherpa family, the

Happy House inn is simple yet charming, with ten beautifully appointed rooms. The highlight? The delicious home-cooked Nepalese cuisine using fresh, locally sourced ingredients from their own organic garden. After a day of exploration, unwind in the cosy living room with its inviting fireplaces. Browse the library, find peace in the meditation/yoga centre or enjoy a drink at the bar. For ultimate relaxation, a candlelit massage room offers Ayurvedic and other rejuvenating therapies.

€€
From €250 / US$272 per night per person on all inclusive.

150 HOTELS YOU NEED TO VISIT BEFORE YOU DIE

NEPAL	Lower Mustang	OFF-THE-MAP
	Jomsom	SANCTUARY

◆ TO VISIT BEFORE YOU DIE BECAUSE

This is the first luxury hotel in one of the world's last uncharted and mystical regions.

Before 2019, exploring the remote Mustang region in Nepal meant weary travellers staying in basic teahouses – often lacking electricity and hot water. Now, the stunning Shinta Mani, designed by Bill Bensley, offers a luxurious alternative. This haven reflects the rich Tibetan heritage in its cuisine, art and decor. Earthen tones and locally sourced materials like hand-hewn wood and Himalayan rock create a warm ambience. Each of the 29 suites boasts floor-to-ceiling windows framing breathtaking views of the Nilgiri range across the valley.

Shinta Mani serves as a perfect gateway to explore Lower Mustang's natural wonders, traditional villages, and monasteries dangling on sheer cliffs. Mustang is one of the world's few almost entirely Buddhist regions, making it a very special place to travel to. After a day of exploration – and often hiking – unwind at the spa with restorative treatments inspired by traditional Himalayan wellness practices.

€€€€
From €1,650 / US$1,797 per room, per night on all inclusive (including activities and permits).

— 63 —
ALILA
JABAL AKHDAR

Al Hajar Mountains
Jabal Akhdar

OMAN

HOT DESERT

◆ TO VISIT BEFORE YOU DIE BECAUSE

This romantic and remote hotel is the perfect spot to recharge and relax without distractions.

Stunningly perched 2,000 metres (6,560 feet) above sea level on the edge of a ravine, this hotel is one of the most daring projects in the Middle East. Located in a secret corner of the Al Hajar Mountains, a three-hour drive from Muscat airport, the hotel is accessible by four-wheel drive only. The villages in this region feel almost Mediterranean, with fruit orchards and green meadows supplied with water from small, artificial irrigation systems.

The hotel is built from local stone and wood that blend into the landscape. The 78 suites vary from the standard Mountain View to two huge villas, each with two bedrooms and a private pool. The style is calm and clean abundant use of dark woods, soft tones, and local arts and crafts.

€€
From €230 / US$260 per night for a double room, full board.

www.alilahotels.com/jabalakhdar

122

SAUDI ARABIA	**Medina Province** Jabal Ithmah Mountains	UNEXPLORED TERRITORY

◆ TO VISIT BEFORE YOU DIE BECAUSE

A country once closed to tourists now has this fabulous desert gem.

Hidden between the dramatic sandstone canyons of northwestern Saudi Arabia, Alula is a UNESCO World Heritage Site and a hidden gem waiting to be explored. This ancient oasis town, located on the former incense trade route in the Medina Province roughly 1,100 kilometres southwest of Riyadh, is often referred to as 'the sister city of Petra' due to its intricate carvings and tombs. In 2021, Our Habitas Alula opened its doors to a sustainable and extraordinary desert resort offering eco-conscious accommodations gently placed amidst the natural, desert scenery. Stay in one of 98 villas: the Celestial and Canyon Art Villas offer other-worldly views of the desert landscape, while the Arabian Villas provide seclusion and breathtaking vistas of the Ashar Valley. To do: go on a guided hike, stargaze – with telescopes – under the vast desert sky, relax beside the super Instagrammable pool and try typical Arabian cuisine in the beautiful Tama Restaurant.

€€
From €250 / US$272 per room, per night.

SINGAPORE	Singapore Beach Road	EXOTIC LEGEND

◆ TO VISIT BEFORE YOU DIE BECAUSE

This is the epitome of the exotic and very glamorous Far East in a bright and buzzy urban setting.

This legendary hotel opened in 1887 and is named after Sir Stamford Raffles, the founder of modern-day Singapore. The hotel recently reopened after a two-year facelift, now with a fresher look, while maintaining its colonial, old-world grandness. There are 115 suites to choose from, from the Studio Suites to the State Room Suite in the historic Bras Basah Wing, all with teakwood flooring and some with verandas and typical rattan chairs. Breakfast here is probably the most lavish morning spread in town. Don't forget to try the Singapore Sling cocktail at the Writers Bar where the current cocktail menu is inspired by Pico Iyer, the bar's first writer-in-residence.

€€
From €380 / US$425 per night with breakfast.

www.raffles.com/singapore

— 66 —
AMANGALLA

SRI LANKA

Galle
Colonial invigoration

AFFORDABLE
ELEGANCE

◆ TO VISIT BEFORE YOU DIE BECAUSE

This is probably one of the most beautiful, small scale, colonial hotel in the whole of Asia.

Set right within the UNESCO-protected Galle Fort in Sri Lanka, Amangalla is a little diamond to stay and experience, very different than any other hotel on the island. Originally built over 200 years ago, first as the headquarters for Dutch commanders and their staff, and then as the New Oriental Hotel, Aman Resorts made sure to restore it with a blend of colonial heritage and contemporary indulgence. With just 29 guest rooms and suites, Amangalla is all about a stay that evokes the colonial times but connects in a gentle way with the modern world. A big charm is the beautiful veranda, with views over the animated streets of the port town. Here Sri Lankan delights are served, presented on vintage plates, a subtle nod to the hotel's rich past. Afternoon cream tea is another included treat, adding to the sense of refined elegance. Want to relax? Head to the beautiful spa or beautiful courtyard swimming pool, which is perfect after exploring Galle with its tiny streets filled with boutique shops and charming eateries.

€€€
From €700 / US$752, for a double room, per night with breakfast, high noon tea and mini bar included.

www.aman.com/resorts/amangalla

150 HOTELS YOU NEED TO VISIT BEFORE YOU DIE

SRI LANKA

Unawatuna

Eluwila

BAREFOOT
JUNGLE RETREAT

◆ TO VISIT BEFORE YOU DIE BECAUSE

This is a relaxing and stylish jungle retreat that doesn't break the bank.

Take a free 10-minute tuk-tuk ride from the historic – and touristy – Dutch colonial seaside town of Galle and nearby Wijaya Beach with its shallow waters to this secret hideaway located on a private island. This sleek ecolodge, nestled amidst a lush island jungle just off the beaten path, offers a haven of relaxation without sacrificing proximity. There are seven bamboo cabins with open-air elements so that birdsong and temple chants become your morning alarm. In the middle of the untamed rainforest is a stunning open-plan restaurant serving tasteful but light and local fare. A rooftop yoga platform and pool overlooking the lawn complete the picture and are perfect for all kinds of wellness retreats often happening at Kaju Green.

€
From €140 / US$150 per night for a double room with breakfast.

AMANPURI

THAILAND	**Phuket**	ICONIC
	Pansea Beach	TRENDSETTER

◆ TO VISIT BEFORE YOU DIE BECAUSE

This hotel set the standard for what would later become the boutique resort hotel.

Amanpuri was the brainchild of leading hotelier Adrian Zecha who, with the opening of this property and the launch of Aman Resorts in 1988, set a new standard for small-scale, luxurious boutique hotels. Thirty years later, Amanpuri, tucked away in the lush jungle of Pansea Beach in Phuket, is still a favourite among the rich and famous, including A-list celebrities. The main centre is a majestic Thai pavilion looking out over a vast, black-tiled pool and in the distance the glistering Andaman Sea. Bed down in one of the 40 private pavilions with shiny wooden floors, sliding doors and a clean, contemporary aesthetic that is the Aman Resorts trademark.

€€€
From €750 / US$840 per night for a double room, with breakfast and private airport transfers.

www.aman.com/resorts/amanpuri

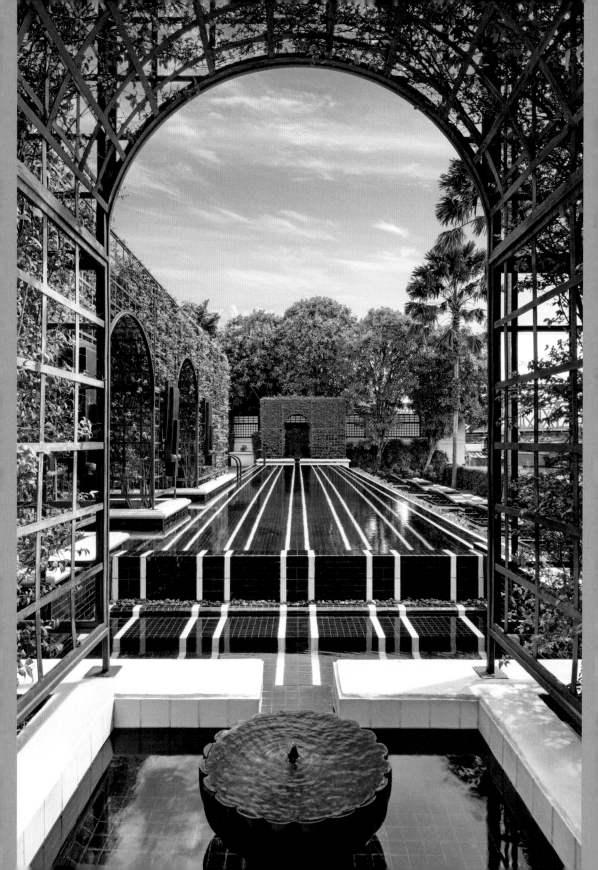

THAILAND

Bangkok
Bang Krabue

**ART DECO
HERITAGE**

◆ TO VISIT BEFORE YOU DIE BECAUSE

With its striking architecture, this may well be Bangkok's best and most beautiful hotel.

Designed by renowned hotel guru and designer Bill Bensley, The Siam has its own special heritage style. Airy and vast marble corridors are arranged around a central courtyard with beautiful tropical plants and plenty of natural light pouring in. The 28 suites all have high wooden ceilings, massive beds and oversized bathrooms with stylish soaker tubs. Another stunning detail is the many antique pieces, even in the rooms, from Buddha statues to original artwork and 19th- and early 20th-century documents and photographs. The Chon Thai restaurant offers classic Thai haute cuisine by the banks of the Chao Phraya while the Deco Bar and Bistro serves classic Western fare and a wide selection of healthy dishes.

€€
From €320 / US$360 per night for a double room, with breakfast.

THAILAND	Bangkok	OLD-WORLD
	South Sathorn	CHARM

◆ TO VISIT BEFORE YOU DIE BECAUSE

This affordable yet opulent hotel mixes colonial with Thai style like no other.

This might be the best hotel in Bangkok for those looking for authenticity and a serious dash of luxury. Despite its size – there are 214 rooms and suites – the hotel still feels like a haven of tranquility and calmness in a hectic city. The rather large rooms and colonial-era suites are furnished with teakwood and beautiful Thai textiles and include spacious bathrooms with wooden floors and large tubs. There's plenty of fine-dining options around the hotel. The romantic Celadon offers classic Thai cuisine served in a pavilion that floats in a pond filled with lotus flowers, and the popular Sunday brunch is a true classic loved by locals and visitors alike.

€
From €140 / US$160 per night for a double room, with breakfast.

VIETNAM	Mekong Delta Can Tho	AFFORDABLE ELEGANCY

◆ TO VISIT BEFORE YOU DIE BECAUSE

This is one of the most stylish and affordable hotels in South East Asia.

Situated on Au Islet, a private island of 21 hectares on the Hau River, a main tributary of the Mekong River, Azerai is still one of the best kept secrets in Southeast Asia. The hotel is only accessible by boat and is a world away from the humdrum of Can Tho city. Hidden among native mangroves and banyan trees sit 60 villas with wide terraces from which to enjoy sunset views overlooking the lake, river and gardens.

Bamboo, rattan and timber feature to bring earthy outdoor tones into the interiors. The ambiance and decor is in the true, refined style of Adrian Zecha, the founder of famed Aman Resorts who is set to debut this new hotel brand and hotel along the Mekong Delta.

€
Rates star from €210 / US$235 per night, B&B.

azerai.com/azerai-can-tho

— 72 —
HAUS HIRT

AUSTRIA

Salzburger Land
Bad Gastein

**ALPINE
THERMAL SPA**

◆ TO VISIT BEFORE YOU DIE BECAUSE

This is probably the cosiest and most intimate small hotel in the Austrian Alps.

When Evelyn Ikrath bought this old spa hotel in 2000, she wanted to keep the spirit of the 1920s, while spicing it up so that Haus Hirt would become one of the most welcoming Alpine inns in Austria. The eccentric hotel, with 29 rooms, large windows and wooden balconies floating above the Gastein Valley, used to receive guests the likes of Thomas Mann, Lady Churchill and the Shah of Persia. Now, the ever-present Evelyn hosts an international clientele that keeps returning for her warm hospitality and attention to detail. Evelyn commissioned a DJ friend to come up with dedicated playlists that set the mood and vibe throughout the day. In the lounge, contemporary art blends well with the eclectic features and decor of the old building. The perfect place to read a good book after a day of skiing or when the Gastein Valley gets snowed under.

€
From €110 / US$125 per person per night, half board.

www.haus-hirt.com/en

— 73 —
HOTEL GASTHOF HIRSCHEN SCHWARZENBERG

AUSTRIA

Vorarlberg
Bregenzerwald

UNTOUCHED
BY TIME

◆ TO VISIT BEFORE YOU DIE BECAUSE

Traditional Austrian inn owned by the same family for generations.

Many things at the 265-year-old Hirschen Schwarzenberg have stayed the same for centuries, while other things are ahead of their time, mainly thanks to young Peter Fetz, the fifth generation of his family to own it. Located in the picturesque village of Bregenzerwald, this traditional inn is built in baroque style in age-old, weathered wood. Inside, the Stube is probably the most romantic eatery in this corner of Austria. Organic, Austrian wines are paired with the inventive but down-to-earth cuisine of Jonathan Burger, the young, creative head chef who loves local products and the culinary heritage of this region. Upstairs are some of the inn's 36 rooms, while the rest are located in the traditionally built 'Wälderhaus' House of the Forests directly behind the main house. They have been occupied by all kinds of individuals, including artists, royals and gourmets, who prefer perfection and tradition to new and trendy.

€
From €150 / US$170 per night with breakfast.

BERGDORF PRIESTEREGG

AUSTRIA

Salzburger Land
Leogang

**FROM PASTURE
TO BED AND TABLE**

◆ TO VISIT BEFORE YOU DIE BECAUSE

Sometimes a traditional Alpine chalet is so much cosier than a soulless design hotel.

The quintessential Bergdorf Priesteregg is owned by Renate and Huwi Oberlader, former farmers who wanted to transform their huge piece of farmland, located at an altitude of 1,100 metres in Saalfelden-Leogang, into something unusual. Bergdorf Priesteregg is more than a hotel; it's a private mountain village. In the centre of the village are a pond, wooden benches and sheepskin-covered chairs, and once a week fresh bread is baked in a traditional outdoor oven. The chalets are dotted around this hub, some with two bedrooms, others more luxurious, such as the Luis Trenker and the Villa Etaner, which have more space and a private swimming pool. A cosy restaurant and bar serves traditional dishes, from perfectly grilled steaks to delicious cheese-based specials.

€€
From €275 / US$310 per person per night, with breakfast.

JAGDSCHLOSS HOTEL

AUSTRIA	Tyrol	IMPERIAL WELCOME
	Kühtai	IN THE ALPS

◆ TO VISIT BEFORE YOU DIE BECAUSE

This is Austria's most classic and iconic Schlosshotel with a wealth of charm and character.

Check into the charismatic and historic Jagdschloss Hotel owned by the Count of Stolberg-Stolberg and discover Kühtai, a tranquil and relatively unknown skiing village high in the snowy mountains of the Austrian Tyrol. The count's father inherited the 30-acre (12-hectare) domain at birth from his mother, the granddaughter of Franz Josef I and Elisabeth of Bavaria, aka Sisi, and converted the royal residence into a lodge in the 1950s. This is not a classic ski hotel; guests come here to rest, to read a good book beside the fire, to meet people and to enjoy the sunshine and the quiet. The long and aristocratic history of the house is tangible: the creaking floorboards, the red-and-white striped Habsburg shutters and downstairs the wonderful Fürstenstube (Prince's Lounge), the heart of the house, where most people come together, meet and possibly become friends for life. It's no wonder the count's motto for the hotel is 'come as a guest and leave as a friend'.

€
From €180 / US$200 per night with breakfast.

BELGIUM	Antwerp	HOMELY
	't Groen Kwartier	ELEGANCE

◆ TO VISIT BEFORE YOU DIE BECAUSE

Once you check into this elegant sanctuary, you won't want to check out.

Housed in a former Augustinian convent, August has 44 rooms and suites spread across five historical buildings. No two rooms are the same; the smaller rooms are in the former nuns' convent, while the larger rooms are located below the dark wooden ceiling on the top floor where you can hide away from the world. The exterior, in neo-Flemish Renaissance and neo-Baroque style, contrasts beautifully with the neutral, almost sacral interior with comfortable furniture, custom-made by Molteni&C, and designed to create a homely feel by renowned Belgian architect Vincent Van Duysen. The serenity of the bedrooms gives way to a lively and buzzy atmosphere downstairs where the bar serves drinks and food from 11am until to 11pm, and the menu is designed by two-Michelin-starred chef Nick Brill.

€
From €140 / US$160 per night for a double room.

www.august-antwerp.com

HOTEL VAN CLEEF

BELGIUM	West-Flanders Bruges	ECLECTIC LUXURY

◆ TO VISIT BEFORE YOU DIE BECAUSE

Nowhere beats the peaceful ambience and relaxing atmosphere of this romantic getaway.

Located next to the uber-romantic waterways of Bruges, Hotel Van Cleef spills out onto a garden and sunny terrace that overlook a lovely stretch of canal and the medieval city. The hotel is an eccentric mix of styles and themes, all elegantly merged into one grand old building with high ceilings and tall windows. Some rooms are small and cosy while others are big and decorated with luxury brands such as Hermès and Missoni, giving them extra cachet. The breakfast is pretty amazing and the best spot is the classic bar where you can sit and sip your complimentary glass of champagne.

€€
From €265 / US$300 per night for a double room, with breakfast.

www.hotelvancleef.be

DENMARK	Bornholm	DANISH ISLAND
	Allinge	REFUGE

◆ TO VISIT BEFORE YOU DIE BECAUSE

There is nothing like waking up to wide-open views over the Baltic Sea in a Scandi-chic setting.

Bornholm has fast become the absolute foodie island destination in Scandinavia, just a hop away from Copenhagen. Hotel Nordlandet is the island's first boutique hotel, opened by Danish entrepreneur Martin Smidt Kristensen in 2015. With a huge panoramic terrace overlooking the sea, the restaurant serves a new, casual-style Nordic cuisine presented by top chef Nicolai Nørregaard from Michelin-starred restaurant Kadeau in Copenhagen and its sister restaurant with the same name in Bornholm. All dishes are presented on simple plates made by local ceramicist Lov i Listed. Menu items reference the land and sea, and are perfect washed down with a local craft beer. The rooms are scattered throughout the old villa and the new adjoining building, all with wide-open views over the Baltic Sea and the rocks in front of this romantic hotel.

€
From €150 / US$170 for a double room with breakfast.

RADISSON COLLECTION ROYAL HOTEL

DENMARK	Copenhagen	PIONEERING
	Tivoli Gardens	DESIGN

◆ TO VISIT BEFORE YOU DIE BECAUSE

This was the world's first design hotel, still very relevant and incredibly sexy.

When the Radisson SAS Royal opened its doors in 1960 it was iconic in many ways. It was the first skyscraper in Copenhagen, the highest building in Scandinavia and the first ever design hotel, where Arne Jacobsen took care of almost every detail, from the look of the 20-storey glass-and-steel facade to the sleek cutlery and iconic Egg and Swan chairs. With views of the Tivoli Gardens and the Baltic Sea in the distance, the Royal (now called the Radisson Collection Royal Hotel) boasts the best location in Copenhagen. In 2018, the Royal, with its 261 rooms (our favourite is the corner Club Room), underwent a serious facelift with the help of local design company Space Copenhagen, leaving Jacobsen's spirit intact but adding some new touches and details in line with this building's design pedigree. If you don't like the new look, book room number 606 for a night of design history in a room that still retains all of Jacobsen's original designs.

€
From €190 / US$215 for a double room with breakfast.

www.radissonhotels.com/en-us/hotels/radisson-collection-copenhagen

DENMARK	Jutland	NORDIC
	Ebeltoft	SEASIDE ESCAPE

◆ TO VISIT BEFORE YOU DIE BECAUSE

This is a beautifully restored traditional *badehotel* with a serious Nordic vibe.

The Danish Riviera beckons! Denmark's Jutland peninsula boasts a charming seaside village called Ebeltoft, where you'll find Langhoff & Juul, a boutique hotel brimming with Nordic charm. This former 'badehotel' mixes minimalist design with captivating Kattegat Sea views. The 35 rooms (including suites and apartments) all have balconies or terraces with views over Ebeltoft Bay where people swim, kayak and even surf. Langhoff & Juul (which also has a wonderful restaurant in Aarhus) is a fine place for gourmands. The onsite restaurant has the freshest, locally sourced ingredients (think hand-peeled shrimps or delicious asparagus), and the views from both inside and the big terrace are magical, especially at sunset. The weekend dinners are legendary, especially on long, balmy summer nights with the calm Ebeltoft Bay right in front of you.

€
From €150 / US$163 per night for a double room with breakfast.

ESTONIA

West Estonian Archipelago
Muhu Island

**BALTIC ISLAND
SANCTUARY**

◆ TO VISIT BEFORE YOU DIE BECAUSE

This grand, perfectly restored manor house is the ultimate Baltic island escape.

Just off the coast of mainland Estonia is the little-known island of Muhu, which until the early 1990s was under Soviet control and cut off from mainland Estonia. Today, Muhu is very welcoming and home to one of the dreamiest castles in Europe: Pädaste Manor, owned by the dynamic Dutchman Martin Breuer and his partner, Imre Sooäär, who was born on Muhu and created this 24-room boutique hotel. The grand house hides a collection of stately but warmly decorated suites on the top floors. Breakfast and dinner are enjoyed in the main dining room with its tall windows that look out onto the wild nature of Muhu. Hidden in the former carpenter's house is another restaurant, the Yacht Club, that serves lunch on the airy terrace with views over the tranquil bay. A real treat is the spa where natural treatments with hay or goat milk butter are perfect after a dip in the wooden hot tub on the edge of the Baltic Sea.

€
From €179 / US$200 per night for a double room, with breakfast.

www.padaste.ee

— 82 —
NORTHERN LIGHTS RANCH

FINLAND

Finnish Lapland
Levi

NORDIC
REFUGE

◆ TO VISIT BEFORE YOU DIE BECAUSE

Watching the Northern Lights from the comfort of your bed is wonderfully magical and unique.

With its 16 Sky View Cabins, the secluded and luxurious Northern Lights Ranch is completely designed to experience the Northern Lights in a dark setting – not only outdoors, but also from the comfort of your cabin bedroom. Each cabin features giant glass windows and a heated glass roof, allowing you to watch the sky do its magic without having to step out into the Arctic cold. Some of the luxury cabins have an outdoor jacuzzi. The Ranch has a bar and a restaurant serving hearty, Finnish dishes, from reindeer steak to grilled local salmon.

€€€
From €545 / US$610 for a Sky View Cabin.

HÔTEL LES ROCHES ROUGES

FRANCE	French Riviera	MODERNIST
	Saint-Raphaël	MED

◆ TO VISIT BEFORE YOU DIE BECAUSE

This hotel captures the essence of the French Riviera: unlimited *joie de vivre* and a relaxed vibe.

In front of Hôtel Les Roches Rouges there's a quintessential Mediterranean beach, surrounded by unspoiled nature, just opposite the beautiful Ile d'Or and hidden between perfumed pine and tamarisk trees. Hôtel Les Roches Rouges is a white beacon built in a true 1950s modernist design. The 47 rooms have a sensitive colour scheme flowing over into the exterior: hues of blue, white, orange and lemon yellow. Everything centre around barefoot Riviera luxury, such as the handful of wooden huts and viewpoints for admiring the sunset and sea, while the Mediterranean garden and natural seawater pool with a swimming lane cut directly into the coastal rock add to the experience. After a game of pétanque go for a Michelin-starred dinner at La Teressa with a magnificent view over the Mediterranean.

€€
From €320 / US$360 per night with breakfast.

— 84 —
LA DIVINE COMÉDIE

FRANCE	Provence	WILD
	Avignon	ROMANCE

◆ TO VISIT BEFORE YOU DIE BECAUSE

This captures Provençal charm in an intimate urban setting.

The five suites at La Divine Comédie take guests on a journey through time, art history and the history of Avignon. During the 14th century, the site on which the property is located played host to Cardinal Amédée de Saluce's private livery, and his entire household – private and professional – lived and worked in the buildings surrounding the property.

Today, this small hotel is all about elegance and classic comfort, a hideaway in charming Avignon amid one of the loveliest private city gardens in the South of France, with a stunning swimming pool included.

€€€
From €350 / US$395 per night for a double room, with breakfast.

www.la-divine-comedie.com

FRANCE	The Alps	BAUHAUS
	Flaine	MOUNTAIN RETREAT

◆ TO VISIT BEFORE YOU DIE BECAUSE

This style of clean minimalist mountain architecture is one of a kind.

Terminal Neige opened its doors in December 2016, in line with Flaine's 1960s Bauhaus architecture and Marcel Breuer's minimalist style. The expansive lobby of this super family friendly hotel transforms into a vibrant space where different generations come together. Fabrics in bold Amerindian patterns, a crackling fireplace, and a captivating mix of street art alongside a Dubuffet masterpiece create a welcoming ambiance. Terminal Neige has 98 rooms with concrete, wool and chestnut-wood furniture designed by Jean-Louis and Nicolas Sibuet. A 'friendly kitchen' concept offers generous buffets for breakfast served on the sunny terrace, inventive lunch dishes with open tartines and the most famous hearty snack on the ski slopes in France, the *burger of the peaks*.

€
From €150 / US$170 per night with breakfast.

FRANCE	**French Riviera** La Croix Valmer	THE NEW CÔTE D'AZUR STYLE

◆ TO VISIT BEFORE YOU DIE BECAUSE
This is a good example of the new and fresh Cote d'Azur style of hotels.

This delightful boutique hotel, designed by renowned architect Philippe Starck, proves that the Côte d'Azur can be fun, relaxed and fresh, offering an alternative to the classic options along the coast. Lily of the Valley has 46 guest rooms and suites, each with spectacular views of the sparkling sea and a pretty coastline dotted with swathes of lavender, rosemary and Aleppo pine trees. True to Starck's style, all rooms feature minimalist aesthetics and high-end amenities. Guests can unwind at the Shiseido Spa, relax by the two outdoor swimming pools, play a game of tennis, or join one of the hotel's health programmes, from detoxing to weight loss. Hop on the complimentary shuttle to the nearby Plage de Gigaro, where the hotel has a private beach club offering water sports (try a classic windsurfing lesson or use the giant paddleboards), plus luxurious sun loungers, chic cabanas and two dreamy restaurants, La Plage and La Terrasse, situated right at the water's edge.

€€
From €380 / US$413 for a double room with breakfast.

www.lilyofthevalley.com

150 HOTELS YOU NEED TO VISIT BEFORE YOU DIE

MAISON PROUST

FRANCE	Paris Le Marais	A NOVEL HOTEL

◆ TO VISIT BEFORE YOU DIE BECAUSE
This is Paris's most romantic and plush boutique hotel with a quaint theme.

Parisian elegance meets literary inspiration at Maison Proust, a five-star boutique hotel set back on a quiet street in Le Marais. In this gorgeously restored six-storey townhouse, the hotel pays homage to the life and works of Marcel Proust, author of the monumental novel *Remembrance of Things Past*. Guests are immediately caught up in the enchantment with the sumptuously furnished Belle Époque salon as the biggest eye-catcher. This intimate haven boasts just 23 uniquely decorated rooms and suites, each inspired by a character or theme from Proust's masterpiece. Expect to find plush fabrics, curated artwork and subtle nods to the Belle Époque era. Many rooms offer private balconies overlooking the charming Parisian streets. Downstairs is the elegant La Mer Spa with a huge, Arabian-style swimming pool, decorated by the craftsmen from the palaces of the King of Morocco.

€€€
From €1,000 / US$1,089 per night for a double room with breakfast.

GEORGIA	**Caucasus Mountains** Kazbegi	SECRET MOUNTAIN INN

◆ TO VISIT BEFORE YOU DIE BECAUSE

This hotel is located in one of Europe's best-kept secrets for lovers of dramatic mountain scenery.

A converted former Soviet sanatorium, this hotel feels like the Soho House private members club in the dramatic Caucasus mountain range, whose peaks rise to a daunting 5,000 metres (16,400 feet) providing a spectacular backdrop for this retreat in northern Georgia. Hotel Kazbegi has 155 guestrooms, all with breathtaking vistas. The drama outside is soothed inside by the warmth of wood, glass and steel. A restaurant serving traditional

Georgian fare interspersed with a host of international dishes is accompanied by a cosy bar with a fireplace and a cigar menu. Meanwhile, a sweeping sun terrace provides a place to relax and soak up the rugged surroundings. A stunning place to go hiking, quad-biking or heliskiing in winter, with jaw-dropping views of Mount Kazbek.

€
From €130 / US$145 per night with breakfast.

www.roomshotels.com/kazbegi

GERMANY	Berlin	ANIMAL
	Tiergarten	DELUXE

◆ TO VISIT BEFORE YOU DIE BECAUSE

This is the new style Berlin where elegance meets craziness, thanks to the private access to the world-famous Zoological Garden.

When Das Stue opened a stone's throw from the Tiergarten Park in Berlin, this hotel set a new standard for the rebellious city. Das Stue means 'living room' in Danish and the concept of this luxury abode is that of stylish living where people come together to relax and enjoy themselves. The hotel, tucked away in an elegant old building that was formerly the Danish Embassy, has 80 rooms, a lounge with bar and an outdoor terrace. Guests have private access to the Berlin Zoological Garden right next door. Spanish chef Paco Perez takes care of the hotel's two restaurants, one of which earned him his fifth Michelin star.

€€
From €183 / US$200 per night for a double room, breakfast and picnic included.

| GERMANY | Bavarian Alps
Krün | ELEGANTLY
PEACEFUL |

◆ TO VISIT BEFORE YOU DIE BECAUSE

Although it is located in a silent, picturesque wood, this is one of Germany's powerhouse hotels.

Despite its secluded natural setting, Schloss Elmau has a fascinating history and has welcomed many high-ranking and well-known guests. This high-end retreat hosted the G7 Summit in 2015, when Obama declared it to be one of the most beautiful castle hotels in Europe. Built in 1916, the original castle was almost entirely destroyed by a fire in 2005, but today Schloss Elmau has a super-cosy and classic decor with hardwood floors and deep, warm colours. All rooms have extensive views over the Bavarian Alps, which can also be seen from the bar's terrace, perfect for an apéritif before heading to one of ten restaurants choose from Bavarian mountain cheese fondue in the charming Kaminstüberl to healthy Asian options.

€€€
From €530 / US$595 per night for a double room, breakfast and picnic included.

www.schloss-elmau.de/en

GREECE	**Crete** Elounda Bay	ICON IN THE MED

◆ TO VISIT BEFORE YOU DIE BECAUSE

Ancient Greek heritage mixes with modern elegance for a top Cretan escape.

Reborn from the ashes of the iconic Blue Palace hotel, the Phāea Blue Palace opened up again along the Cretan coastline in the spring of 2024. The concept of the reimagined hotel is clear: downsizing and upgrading to create an even more exclusive Greek experience. Phāea Blue Palace now has a mere 47 bungalows and suites and one stunning private villa. The decor is all about island aesthetics, with natural materials, splashes of Aegean blues and locally sourced artwork on the walls. The location is also still incredible: nestled between the bijou fishing village of Plaka and the chic port of Elounda, both perfect for exploring and experiencing the local lifestyle. Once back at the hotel, the farm-to-table feasts are lovely, as are the cooking classes led by culinary masters, while the Phāea Spa is inspired by ancient Greek practices and infused with local botanicals. Nothing better than ending a perfect day in the Med with a Cretan massage.

€€
From €290 / US$315 for a double room with breakfast.

— 92 —
MONUMENT HOTEL

GREECE

Athens
Psirri

GRAND
ELEGANCE

◆ TO VISIT BEFORE YOU DIE BECAUSE

An intimate and small boutique hotel can also feel grand and monumental.

It's back to the bygone, grand era of Athens's past when stepping through the grand entrance of this newly opened boutique hotel. This 19th-century mansion, originally a merchant's residence, was restored after years of neglect into a luxurious boutique hotel with just nine guest rooms and suites. Soaring ceilings, intricate paintings, and vast windows overlooking a charming Athenian scene set the tone. The modern bathrooms are cleverly concealed in mirrored boxes, maximising the airy space. The decor is understated yet luxurious, featuring bespoke furniture and statement pieces by renowned Scandinavian brands. While breakfast is the only meal served, it's a gourmet affair showcasing fresh, local ingredients. You can also mix your own drinks from the bar or have cocktails delivered to your room. In the basement there is a complimentary sauna and steam room with a single treatment room offering rejuvenating massages using Greek essential oils.

€€
From €250 / $272 per night for a double room with breakfast.

https://www.monumenthotelathens.com

GREECE	Cyclades	THE GREEK
	Antiparos	ISLAND ESCAPE

TO VISIT BEFORE YOU DIE BECAUSE
This is the definition of a luxury boutique hotel in Greece.

The Rooster, hidden away on the quieter Cycladic island of Antiparos, embraces a perfect 'low-profile, high-privacy' ethos. The charming and eccentric owner, Mrs Athanasia Comninos, prioritises slowing down and savouring simple pleasures over packed itineraries while on holiday. The spa treatments and therapies focus on restoring both body and mind. The Rooster features 16 spacious houses, some with their own pool. It's almost like owning your own chic abode in Greece. Think exclusive Greek island home: leafy terraces, local woven accents, curated coffee table books, private pools. Families can enjoy the Farmhouse, nestled amidst fragrant gardens away from the main building. The philosophy here is all about simplicity and balance, even if it's just lingering over a long lunch with Mediterranean views, savouring farm-fresh Greek salads or enjoying cocktails under the stars.

€€€€
From €990 / US$1,078 for a private house with breakfast.

GREECE	Cyclades	GREEK ISLAND
	Sifnos	THERAPY

◆ TO VISIT BEFORE YOU DIE BECAUSE

This place is brimming with *philoxenia*, the 'love of visitors' that embodies Greek hospitality.

Greek owner Isidora Chandeli and her husband, Miltos, who grew up spending their summers on Sifnos, share a passion for this Cycladic island. You'll find their beautiful boutique hotel perched atop a cliff overlooking the Aegean Sea. Built in the traditional whitewashed style with pops of Aegean blue, Verina has a minimalist look, where natural materials and soothing earth tones create a calming ambience. The 14 rooms, each with a private balcony or terrace, are also perfect for families. The restaurant Bostani (Greek for a small garden in a house) offers local and Aegean dishes served 'at home', right by the stunning pool or in the restaurant itself with fabulous views over the Med.

€
From €170 / US$185 per person, per night
on all inclusive.

verinahotelsifnos.com

150 HOTELS YOU NEED TO VISIT BEFORE YOU DIE

ILIMANAQ LODGE

GREENLAND

Disko Bay
Ilulissat

LESS IS MORE

◆ TO VISIT BEFORE YOU DIE BECAUSE

This is the Arctic end of the world where icebergs float by and whales befriend you.

It's just a 15-minute boat trip from the Greenlandic town of Ilulissat to this modern lodge located in the remote settlement of Ilimanaq. Fifteen wooden A-frame cabins look out over a tranquil bay where icebergs slowly drift by and the occasional whale pops up. All cabins boast floor-to-ceiling windows on two levels so you can watch the majestic Greenlandic landscape from your bed or private terrace. After a long hike or tour of the fjord, meet the locals of Ilimanaq in the lodge restaurant or go dine with them at home and learn about the Greenlandic way of life in such a faraway place beyond the Arctic Circle.

€
From €145 / US$160 per person per night, breakfast and transfers included.

GREENLAND	West Coast	AN ARCTIC
	Disko Bay/Nuuk	RETREAT

◆ TO VISIT BEFORE YOU DIE BECAUSE
This is the purest way to experience the remote Arctic.

In 2017, Jon and Anika Krogh, a dynamic Danish-Greenlandic couple, opened two of the most beautiful mobile tent camps in Greenland, offering an all-inclusive and exclusive experience. This is luxury wilderness: bedding down in comfortable and spacious canvas tents with private bathrooms, overlooking deep, quiet bays where small icebergs or whales can be spotted. There is Camp Saqqaq in Disko Bay and Camp Kiattua near the capital Nuuk. From June to September, activities include setting foot on a floating iceberg, embarking on invigorating hikes, or simply exploring the untouched landscape in quiet contemplation. After each adventure, it's all about unwinding in the hot tub and savouring delicious homemade dishes served in the communal tipi tent, surrounded by fellow nature lovers who share your appreciation for remote and pristine environments.

€€€€
From €1,750 / US$1,906 per person per day
on full board, with boat transfers included.

www.nomadgreenland.com

ICELAND	**Snæfellsnes**	VOLCANIC
	Budir	SETTING

◆ TO VISIT BEFORE YOU DIE BECAUSE

The views from this hotel are what Iceland is all about: beautiful extremes and extreme beauty.

With the Atlantic literally a few metre away, Hótel Búðir is perhaps the only real beachfront hotel in Iceland. It lies next to a lava field, with views over the Snæfellsjökull glacier, and on a summer's evening – when there are bonfire parties on the beach and guests go swimming – this hotel is a surreal place. With its large windows, guests can take in the natural beauty of the surroundings from the comfort of their lounge, where in winter an open fire keeps them warm during the cold Icelandic nights.

€
From €130 / US$145 per night for a double room, all inclusive, including activities and transfers.

— 98—
ELEVEN DEPLAR FARM

ICELAND

Troll Peninsula
Fljót Valley

OFF-THE-GRID
LUXURY

◆ TO VISIT BEFORE YOU DIE BECAUSE

This is the most luxurious property in Iceland, blissfully remote and secluded.

In a secluded valley, about a 90-min drive from Akureyri Airport, lies this old sheep farm, converted into the most luxurious hotel this close to the Arctic Circle. Deplar Farm has only 13 suites all looking out onto a tranquil landscape, often snowed under or enchanted by the Northern Lights in winter. The traditional black timber houses with their turf-topped roofs are perfectly complemented by the contemporary floor-to-ceiling windows, offering magnificent views over the valley. The hotel has a spa with a geothermal indoor/outdoor pool and an outdoor Viking sauna.

€€€
From €2,350 / US$2,640 per night for a double room, all inclusive, including all activities and transfers.

www.elevenexperience.com/deplar-farm-iceland-winter

ICELAND

Highlands
Kerlingarfjöll Mountains

AN ELEVATED EXPERIENCE

◆ TO VISIT BEFORE YOU DIE BECAUSE

You need to jump in a super jeep to get to this remote gem.

When a hotel transfer becomes an experience: this extremely remote lodge is only accessible by 4x4 super jeep and a three-hour scenic drive from Reykjavik to Kerlingarfjöll, a volcanic mountain range at an altitude of almost 1,500 metres. Set amidst Central Iceland's isolated highlands, where two glaciers are the protagonist, sits Highland Base, the first luxury hotel in Iceland's wild mountain range. Highland Base has a main building with 28 rooms and suites, as well as six cosy lodges, each with grand floor-to-ceiling windows that reveal the raw beauty of the surrounding mountains.

The two biggest suites have private terraces with soothing hot tubs for admiring the Northern Lights or the midnight sun. Underground passages transport guests from the suites to the inviting restaurant and bar with its warm Icelandic hospitality or the beautiful spa with geothermal baths and saunas. Open year-round, Highland Base takes its guests on summery hikes or wintery snowmobiling and thrilling skiing adventures.

€€€
Double room from €400 / US$430 per night.

www.highlandbase.is

— 100 —
THE RETREAT
AT BLUE LAGOON

ICELAND

Reykjanes Peninsula
Grindavík

A DREAM-
COME-TRUE STAY

TO VISIT BEFORE YOU DIE BECAUSE

You can skip the crowds at this blockbuster attraction and have it all to yourself.

The popular bucket list experience of dipping a toe in the world-famous Blue Lagoon in Iceland can be taken to a next and much more private level by booking a room at The Retreat, the newish and sleek hotel at the Blue Lagoon. There are 62 suites that almost melt into the charcoal black, volcanic landscape created by a 755-year-old lava flow. Think floor-to-ceiling windows boasting spectacular views of the milky-blue lagoon, accessible directly from some suites via private balconies. Lovely details include the heated bathroom floors and in-room tablets to order incredible spa treatments after a relaxing swim in the geothermal water. Another treat is the Moss Restaurant, again with panoramic lagoon views, serving exquisite cuisine crafted with fresh, local ingredients.

€€€€
From €1,466 / US$1,596 per night for a suite.

www.bluelagoon.com/accommodation/retreat-hotel

— 101 —
ADARE MANOR

IRELAND

Limerick
Adare

STATELY
GRANDEUR

◆ TO VISIT BEFORE YOU DIE BECAUSE

Connoisseurs claim this is the finest and most beautiful hotel in Ireland, dating back to 1830.

Formerly this was one of the grandest private homes in Ireland with 365 windows, 52 chimneys, seven pillars and four towers representing the seasons. Today, this manor house, completely renovated in 2017, is Ireland's most luxurious hotel with 104 rooms and suites. With its romantic, fairy-tale vibe even in winter, this hotel is the perfect place to hide away with a good book next to a roaring open fire. Adare

Manor has the second-longest dining room in Ireland – inspired by the Hall of Mirrors at Versailles – where you can have a traditional afternoon tea after a long walk in the woods. The Oak Room restaurant has a Michelin star and serves refined dishes using some of Ireland's best ingredients.

€€
From €325 / US$365 per night for a double room, with breakfast.

176

www.adaremanor.com

BREAC.HOUSE

IRELAND	**Donegal** Horn Head	**END OF THE** **WORLD ESCAPE**

◆ TO VISIT BEFORE YOU DIE BECAUSE
To stay here is to experience the wild and wonderful coast of Ireland in style.

There are only three guestrooms at Breac. House and they are named to reflect the experiences guests have at the magical Horn Head. The name of first room, Dulse, refers to the dulse seaweed found on the beach, in the hot tubs and in the scones served with local smoked salmon. The name of another room, Turf, refers to the inescapable smell of turf fires in Donegal and the turf used to smoke the salmon. The whole interior design has been created using locally crafted furniture and local materials such as Fanad granite and Ardara quartzite from a South Donegal quarry. Staying here offers a true Irish experience in a refreshing and casual atmosphere.

€€
From €275 / US$310 per night for a double room, breakfast and picnic included.

ITALY	Amalfi Coast	JAMES BOND
	Positano	ELEGANCE

◆ TO VISIT BEFORE YOU DIE BECAUSE

This is the epitome of Amalfi chic with stunning views from every corner of this fabulous hotel.

Guests keep returning to this hotel which opens up to one of the world's most stunning views of Positano and the Faraglioni rock stacks of Capri. Set high on the cliffs overlooking the Amalfi coastline, Il San Pietro was founded in 1934 by Carlo ('Carlino') Cinque, and thanks to its perfect location and 61 elegant rooms and suites, it has become a favourite spot among many high-profile guests who want to enjoy *dolce far niente* in style. The terrace decor is accented with locally produced hand-painted tiles, making the terrace a perfect spot for an Italian-style aperitivo with the dreamiest views of the Amalfi Coast and glitzy Positano.

€€€
From €395 / US$445 per night for a double room, with breakfast.

— 104 —
IL PELLICANO

ITALY	Tuscany	SEASIDE
	Porto Ercole	GLAM

◆ TO VISIT BEFORE YOU DIE BECAUSE

After staying here, you will want to keep coming back to this laid-back Tuscan seaside resort.

Well-hidden among the cedar groves and lavender and rosemary scrub of the Monte Argentario peninsula, overlooking the turquoise Tyrrhenian Sea, Il Pellicano is the ultimate seaside enclave in Italy. It's not a well-kept secret that the pool deck at the hotel is where the bold and beautiful of Italy and beyond meet during the summer months. Il Pellicano is classic but stylish, with a timeless yet hip and chic atmosphere. The hotel has 50 rooms and suites, each recently renovated with perfect terraces and patios. Dining options include the gourmet Michelin-starred Il Pellicano or the more casual Pelligrill Tuscan Grill, offering Tuscan specialties. A Pelican martini at the hotel's lovely terrace bar ensures a good start to a long and balmy night.

€€
From €347 / US$390 per night for a double room, with breakfast.

www.hotelilpellicano.com

PALAZZO MARGHERITA

ITALY	Basilicata	MEZZOGIORNO
	Bernalda	ELEGANCE

◆ TO VISIT BEFORE YOU DIE BECAUSE

A stay in Sofia Coppola's favourite suite is an epic experience on any Italian odyssey.

Palazzo Margherita is located in Bernalda, a small hilltop town in the unknown but fantastically charming Basilicata region of Southern Italy and just a hop away from the historic town of Matera. The Baroque Palazzo Margherita was once a crumbling 19th-century remnant of more flourishing periods in Italy's south, until Francis Ford Coppola, director of the film series *The Godfather*, discovered it and promised to restore the decaying building to its former glory. Some of the suites were designed by members of the Coppola family, and the end result is more reminiscent of a family retreat than a real hotel, with heavenly, rustic home-made cooking, a relaxed vibe and excellent service with a southern flair.

€€
From €380 / US$429 per night for a double room, with breakfast.

SEXTANTIO ALBERGO DIFFUSO

ITALY

Abruzzo
Santo Stefano di Sessanio

MEDIEVAL REVIVAL

◆ TO VISIT BEFORE YOU DIE BECAUSE

This is the most beautiful and romantic village in Italy far away from the madding crowd.

In the Gran Sasso e Monti della Laga National Park in the Apennine Mountains, the village of Santo Stefano di Sessanio is a well-kept secret. It is surrounded by the incredible beauty of the Abruzzo landscape – reminiscent of New Zealand but with mountain peaks as high as those of the Alps. The massive, ancient stones of the abandoned villages of Abruzzo speak volumes, and narrow passageways and porticos with steps open onto sun-drenched piazzas or a labyrinth of alleyways. Santo Stefano di Sessanio was given a second chance thanks to the vision and bravery of a Swedish-Italian businessman, who created an *albergo diffuso* (a scattered hotel) consisting of hotel rooms distributed over 32 restored village houses. The untouched nature surrounding the village, together with the clever design and meticulous restoration, make this one of the most calming and tranquil places to stay in Europe.

€
From €120 / US$135 per night for a double room, with breakfast.

www.sextantio.it/en/santostefano/abruzzo

IL MONASTERO

ITALY

Tyrrhenian Sea
Ischia

ISLAND
CHARMER

◆ TO VISIT BEFORE YOU DIE BECAUSE
This is the perfect seaside escape for those tired of sterile design hotels.

Ischia's jewel in the crown isn't a gleaming resort, but a charming relic reborn.
A 16th-century castle, accessible by a narrow causeway, offers a unique stay perched high above this beautiful Italian island. Former monks' cells now serve as guest rooms, offering a taste of simple living, yet with vibrant artistry. The 21 rooms have a curated Mediterranean aesthetic with custom-made shelves, wrought-iron beds, and original blue majolica tiles featuring Gabriele Mattera's signature geometric motif. The garden of the old convent is paradisiac with panoramic views of Ischia and a restaurant menu that showcases fresh ingredients grown in the hotel's very own rooftop garden. Just before sunset, the romantic terrace is also the perfect spot for a good old-fashioned Italian *aperitivo momento*.

€
From €130 / US$141 per night for a double room with breakfast.

— 108 —
ROMAZZINO

ITALY

Sardinia
Costa Smeralda

JET-SET
PLAYGROUND

◆ TO VISIT BEFORE YOU DIE BECAUSE

The stunning Costa Smeralda has its most darling hotel queen back.

With waters this blue you'd be forgiven for thinking you're in the Caribbean. But the sculpted, beige cliffs edging the sea are unique to the famous Costa Smeralda in Sardinia. Here, a legendary hotel, the Romazzino, has finally regained its lustre under the prestigious Belmond Hotels label. The resort has a rich history dating back to the 1960s, designed by the prized architect Michele Busiri Vici in a unique, white, Cycladic style. It is a beachside ode to old skool glamour, created by the eccentric Prince Aga Khan, who transformed the Costa Smeralda into a playground for the rich and famous.

Celebrities loved to stay here, often with their megayachts bobbing around in the transparent, Cerulean-blue bay. Romazzino now has 100 rooms, suites and villas, many offering breathtaking views over the sparkling Mediterranean. It's a total seascape here with two refreshing pools, a private beach area, a world-class spa, and a collection of restaurants and bars where you can experience the famous villeggiatura, the Italian art of relaxation.

€€€
From €720 / US$ 784 for a double room
with breakfast.

ITALY	**Sicily** Madonie Mountains	COUNTRY- STYLE CHIC

◆ TO VISIT BEFORE YOU DIE BECAUSE

This is the most stunning farmhouse stay in rural southern Italy.

Think rolling hills and vibrant wildflower meadows tucked away in the hidden Madonie Mountains of Sicily, close to Palermo. Here, a meticulously restored 200-year-old farmhouse, reborn as a boutique hotel in 2018, sits nestled in this idyllic landscape. The farm has 18 spacious rooms and suites, each with private balconies overlooking the extravagant gardens. The decor inside has plenty of rural charm, with some rooms housed in the old winemaker's quarters, others in the former dwellings of the cheesemaker, baker or field guard. Susafa's philosophy centres on slowing down and reconnecting with nature. At the heart of this eco-retreat lies a stunning swimming pool, the perfect spot to unwind after a day of adventure. Hike through the breathtaking scenery or explore the charming villages nestled in the hills. Susafa champions a commitment to green energy, local sourcing (for amazing Sicilian dishes) and waste reduction, so any stay is as green as possible.

€€
From €320 / US$348 for a double room with breakfast.

www.susafa.com

NORWAY	**Sunnmøre** Hjørundfjord	A HISTORIC HIDEAWAY

◆ TO VISIT BEFORE YOU DIE BECAUSE

This is the ultimate, fairytale haunted hotel in the North.

The Sunnmøre Alps are all about dramatic mountains and fairytale fjords. Cascading waterfalls feed crystal lakes and roaring rivers. Winding roads lead to tranquil villages with gingerbread houses and wildflower meadows. Nestled beside the remote Hjørundfjord is Hotel Union Øye, a historic gem since 1891. Its creaky floors whisper tales of Kaiser Wilhelm, Karen Blixen and even Roald Amundsen. Now a Relais & Chateaux property, it boasts 38 rooms and suites. The Blue Room has a captivating local legend and is said to be haunted by a gentle host. Exploring is a must: off-piste skiing in autumn, or hiking and biking Norangsdalen, one of Norway's most beautiful valleys. Après-ski or -hike? Relax on the terrace with waterfall views, warm up by the historic fireplace and enjoy dinner served by friendly staff in traditional attire. Here, dressing elegantly after adventures is still bon ton and only adds to the vibe of this 'end of the world' escape.

€€€
From €320 / US$348 per night.

www.unionoye.no/en

| NORWAY | Svalbard | AN EXTRAORDINARY |
| | Barentsburg | ESCAPE |

TO VISIT BEFORE YOU DIE BECAUSE
There is nothing as invigorating as staying in the heart of the quiet Arctic.

Forget anything conventional at Isfjord Radio Adventure Hotel on the very remote Svalbard archipelago. Nestled on the west coast, this unique retreat breathes new life into a historic radio station built in 1933 in the middle of the Arctic wilderness. Travel with a snow scooter or husky dog sledge through the snowy, mighty mountains of Svalbard with its vast fjords, perfect glaciers and the icy ocean as a constant breathtaking backdrop. The lodge has a strong connection to its special radio station past thanks to a cosy interior with historic exposed beams and vintage details. Isfjord Radio Adventure Hotel has 19 rooms and suites, and an intimate restaurant with a snug lounge and fireplace. Outside there is a hot tub, perfect for witnessing the dancing Northern Lights during the pitch-black nights. In summer you can also travel to the hotel by boat to enjoy the beautiful Arctic nature under that special and constant midnight sun.

€€
From €880 / US$958 per person for a 3-day adventure in summer (with a boat transfer) and breakfast/dinner included.

LITLØY FYR

NORWAY

Vesterålen Archipelago
Litløya Archipelago

A STORMY
ISLAND ESCAPE

◆ Everybody should bed down once in a private lighthouse.

One of these extreme, off-the-map places is Litløy Fyr, a former lighthouse from 1912 transformed into a unique and dreamy escape in the heart of Norway's Vesterålen archipelago. Elena Hansteensen and her partner Frode welcome their guests with warmth and local knowledge. Frode, the expert captain, whisks you away on thrilling RIB boat adventures. While inside it's all about cosying up by the fireplace in one of the three private suites, all with views of the ocean and the Lofoten Mountains painting the horizon with magnificent strokes. The newly opened lighthouse suite, spanning three levels, offers an unforgettable experience. Imagine retreating to your private bedroom, unwinding in the lounge with a crackling fire, or gazing through the glass roof at the star-studded sky. Nothing more than the ambitious Atlantic surrounds this lonely island.

€€€
From €1,700 / US$1,851 for 2 people on 2 nights full board, with boat transfers (30 minutes from the mainland) included.

WOLF LODGE

NORWAY

Troms
Bardu

AN EXCLUSIVE
CLOSE ENCOUNTER

◆ TO VISIT BEFORE YOU DIE BECAUSE
This is a wild and wonderful experience in the High North.

What other hotel website has a moon calendar to help you time your stay? The northernmost wildlife park in the world is also one of the most exclusive – read: only for the happy few. With just a few annual stays available each year, Wolf Lodge offers extreme privacy set deep within the quiet Arctic woods of Northern Norway. Mr Stig Sletten, also known as the wolf whisperer, is Polar Park's master animal guardian and takes the lodge's guests out as their private wildlife guide. The lodge has only three luxurious suites and a private lounge with panoramic windows overlooking the enigmatic wolf enclosure. The rules are a bit similar to an African safari: nobody ventures out alone. Activities include guided hikes, snowmobile races over frozen lakes, spending time with the wolves up close and personal under expert supervision, learning about conservation efforts, and experiencing as a grand finale the Aurora Borealis during winter and the midnight sun in summer. Limited to 15 all-inclusive stays per year with a 3-night minimum, this private lodge offers exclusive access to the wolves and supports their care with its proceeds. Book early – it fills up fast!

€€€€
€68,000 / US$72,941 for 3 nights all inclusive:
all transportation, park experiences, meals and
beverages, as well as additional luxury amenities.

— 114 —
AZORES
WINE COMPANY

PORTUGAL	Azores	VOLCANIC
	Pico Island	GEM

◆ TO VISIT BEFORE YOU DIE BECAUSE

This mini hotel is all about maxi vistas in a pretty and surreal landscape.

In 2014, the Portuguese winemaker António Maçanita set out to revive Pico Island's indigenous grapes and craft the finest wines in the Azores. Alongside colleagues, he braved challenging conditions to establish the Azores Wine Company. The resulting winery, built in 2018, seamlessly blends with the volcanic landscape, designed as a modern homage to traditional Pico *adegas* – it's not just a production facility, but a place to gather, eat and even stay. In 2021, six guest apartments with subdued interiors were added. Large windows showcase the lunar-like landscape, while charred wood and vintage furniture create a warm, inviting atmosphere. The onsite restaurant offers fixed tasting menus with beautiful wine pairings, allowing guests to savour the island's unique wines and great cuisine amidst breathtaking scenery. Go for *petiscos*, small tasting dishes, at the counter, the best spot to try Pico's unique wines.

€
From €180 / US$196 per night for a double room with breakfast.

www.antoniomacanita.com/en/wineries/azores-wine-company

CASA DE SÃO LOURENÇO

PORTUGAL

Serra da Estrela
Manteigas

INTO THE
WILD WOODS

◆ TO VISIT BEFORE YOU DIE BECAUSE

This is a true secret gem in the unknown wild and green heart of
Central Portugal.

Not many travellers are aware of the existence of this wild mountain range located near the Spanish border, offering dramatic, snowy landscapes and a couple of ski slopes during the winter months. Casa de São Lourenço, owned by the well-known Portuguese wool fabrics brand Burel, opened in 2019. This panorama hotel is the only five-star hotel in the Serra da Estrela region with wide-open views over the Glacier Valley. Conceived in 1940 by the architect Rogério de Azevedo

as a *pousada* (inn), Casa de São Lourenço is now a luxury hotel that pays tribute to Portuguese designers, crafts and local products. The floor-to-ceiling windows look out on the landscape and some of the 21 rooms have jaw-dropping views over the Serra. There is a stunning spa and a restaurant that serves authentic cuisine that's full of flavour.

€
From €175 / US$195 per night with breakfast.

www.casadesaolourenco.pt/en

195

HERDADE
DA MALHADINHA NOVA

PORTUGAL

Alentejo
Albernoa

AN ALENTEJAN
SAFARI

◆ TO VISIT BEFORE YOU DIE BECAUSE

This rural retreat tells the heritage story of the Baixo Alentejo in
a contemporary and fresh way.

Driving to the whitewashed gate of
this vast property feels like exploring
an endless, dusty African landscape
with gnarled oak, cork and olive trees
peppering the fields of red earth with
patches of green vines. But this is the
Alentejo: wild, strong and stubborn,
where exceptional hotels like Malhadinha
Nova prove to be a haven of comfort and
luxury, and the perfect base for exploring
this region. The classic and intimate
main country house has six guest rooms,
while new and modern private villas and
guestrooms are scattered throughout the
600-hectare (1,480-acre) property. After
an afternoon of horseback riding, quad
biking or relaxing in the spa, there's wine
tasting, fine dining or lounging in the
evening by the open fire in the comfy
country house with a glass of local wine.

€€
From €300 / US$335 per night with breakfast.

www.malhadinhanova.pt

L'AND VINEYARDS

PORTUGAL   **Alentejo**   ARCHITECTURAL
Montemor-O-Novo   WONDER

◆ TO VISIT BEFORE YOU DIE BECAUSE

Its restorative to bed down amid rustling vineyards with a historic Alentejan town in the distance.

This contemporary retreat is built like an extraordinary white monolith in the vast, wild Alentejo landscape. L'And Vineyards has 26 suites, some with skylights above the beds that enable you to watch the intense, dark night skies of this region. In the main building, the Michelin-starred L'And Vineyards restaurant serves up contemporary takes on local cuisine while the Caudalie Spa downstairs provides a relaxing link between the vineyards outside and the grape-infused treatments inside. The newly opened private holiday house Monte Do Freixo used to be the family's farm but is now one of the most stunning rental houses in Portugal; its interiors feature lots of local elements. The Monte is just a hop away from the hotel and is perfect for guests wanting absolute privacy and views over the untamed Alentejo.

€
From €140 / US$160 per night for a double room, with breakfast.

— 118 —
VERRIDE PALÁCIO SANTA CATARINA

Lisbon

Santa Catarina

URBAN
SOPHISTICATION

◆ TO VISIT BEFORE YOU DIE BECAUSE

This palace hotel is all about low-key luxury and true classic Portuguese craftsmanship.

Next to one of the most iconic viewpoints in the city, the Miradouro de Santa Catarina, this stately *palacio* took years to renovate into one of the most stunning, albeit least known-about, luxury hotels in the city. Although the façade is striking, the real 'wow' effect is in the public spaces and the suites which are all decorated and designed in different styles and vibes, often using Portuguese craftsmanship and local brands – from fresh and airy with light wood and views over the Tagus River (balcony included) to very intimate and romantic in the old historic quarters of the palace. The dining room with small plunge pool is the best location in town to grab breakfast while sitting in the morning sun and enjoying the views over Lisbon.

€€
From €290 / US$325 per night, with breakfast.

— 119 —
FOUR SEASONS HOTEL RITZ LISBON

PORTUGAL

Lisbon
Eduardo VII Park

UNCHANGED
ELEGANCE

◆ TO VISIT BEFORE YOU DIE BECAUSE

Sometimes, instead of new and trendy, all you want is old-school glamour and gorgeous views.

Tired of soulless design hotels? Bed down in the vintage chic Ritz Hotel in Lisbon where old-school glamour blends beautifully with the razzmatazz of the ambitious city outside its walls. The location is perfect, with views, often from a bedroom balcony, over old Lisbon, St. George's Moorish Castle and the Tagus River. The Ritz is the most famous hotel in town, infinitely elegant with immaculate service. It also has the most beautiful rooftop running track (for those tired of generic rooftop bars) with gorgeous vistas over the city. Other attractions include a lovely indoor swimming pool and one of the best hotel spas in the country. Don't miss the amazing breakfast, served outside in the voluptuous garden, perfect for when Lisbon's famous blue sky meets the horizon.

€€
From €660 / US$780 per night for a double room, breakfast included.

www.fourseasons.com/lisbon

SÃO LOURENÇO DE BARROCAL

PORTUGAL

Monsaraz
Alentejo

RURAL SOLITUDE

◆ TO VISIT BEFORE YOU DIE BECAUSE

Staying here is a beautiful compromise between rural authenticity and quiet elegance.

Although this rustic hideaway only opened in 2017, São Lourenço de Barrocal has become one of the most iconic and timeless hotels in Portugal. Located among fields of gnarled cork oaks, vineyards and 2,000-year-old olive trees, this former 780-hectare (1,930-acre) farm estate has been meticulously renovated and restored as a luxury retreat. The estate's owner, José António Uva, who is the eighth generation of his family to live here insisted on carefully preserving the ancient history and family heritage of the monte. He gave architect Eduardo Souto de Moura the task of transforming the age-old cottages, former stables and barns into 40 rooms and studios. On the estate there is also a restaurant with bar, two swimming pools, a Susanne Kaufmann spa and a working farm with horses, which can be hired to explore

€
From €190 / US$215 per night with breakfast.

— 121 —
CORTIJO DEL MARQUÉS

SPAIN

Andalusia
Granada

RURAL
SOLITUDE

◆ TO VISIT BEFORE YOU DIE BECAUSE

This is the perfect place to connect with the Andalusian countryside in style.

Back in the 19th century, more than 30 farming families lived in the Cortijo del Marqués, which, built by a rich marquis, functioned as a small village with its own shops and facilities. Today, an international clientele come here to relax and use the Cortijo as an off-the-map base to explore Granada. In 2010, the Austrian-Dutch couple Roth-Bruggers bought the old farmhouse and decided to trade their successful finance careers

in Hong Kong, London and Madrid for a quieter life in Andalusia. Spread out over the whitewashed Cortijo, the 11 bedrooms are simple yet tastefully decorated, with stunning views over the endless olive tree plantations, perfect for enjoying Andalusia's slow, relaxed lifestyle.

€
From €120 / US$135 per night with breakfast.

www.cortijodelmarques.com

SANT FRANCESC
HOTEL SINGULAR

SPAIN

Balearic Islands

Palma de Mallorca

NOBLE
HOSPITALITY

◆ TO VISIT BEFORE YOU DIE BECAUSE

This stylishly renovated mansion offers a peaceful refuge in Palma's quaint historic quarter.

Book the most beautiful room in Palma de Mallorca: La Torre is the tower suite of Sant Francesc Hotel Singular, situated on multiple levels, with two bedrooms, a living room and private terrace with panoramic views of the old town, the sea and the Tramuntana Mountains. Sant Francesc is hidden in an old manor house once owned by a noble family. The hotel is run by the Soldevila Ferrer family, who since 1918 has run the famous Hotel Majestic in Barcelona. The 42 rooms and suites showcase custom-made furniture, fine antiques and an exclusive contemporary art collection. You can meet at the al fresco Patio Mallorquín for a glass of wine and tapas or at the Singular Restaurant located in the former stables with access to the lush garden. The wonderful rooftop terrace with snack bar and swimming pool is the perfect spot to relax by day, and when the sun goes down the roof is transformed into a starlit lounge and bar.

€
From €170 / US$190 per night with breakfast.

www.hotelsantfrancesc.com

SPAIN	Andalusia	OLD GLAM MED
	Costa del Sol	

◆ TO VISIT BEFORE YOU DIE BECAUSE

Style and substance go hand in hand in this sunny Mediterranean retreat.

Founded by Prince Alfonso of Hohenlohe-Langenberg in 1954, this now legendary resort began its journey as a beautifully rustic beach club attracting the bold and the beautiful. From its humble beginnings as a collection of rooms dotted around a patio and inspired by the then new age of Californian motels, the Marbella Club has evolved over time to include 115 rooms and suites, 14 villas and a variety of restaurants, bars and guest offerings. With its bougainvillea-lined walkways and sun-soaked patios decorated with hand-painted tiles, this retreat resembles a classic Andalusian village.

€€
From €380 / US$425 per night with breakfast.

204

SPAIN	Barcelona	URBAN
	Eixample	COOL CAT

◆ TO VISIT BEFORE YOU DIE BECAUSE

This is the absolute coolest hotel for exploring Barcelona from inside out.

In the elegant Eixample neighbourhood, Casa Bonay is the favourite place to bed down in Barcelona for design enthusiasts and curious travellers. Housed in a perfectly restored 19th-century neoclassical building, Casa Bonay is not only a hotel but also a treasured place for locals to eat and drink. In the evenings, the hotel's ground-floor Libertine bar transforms into a lively scene, perfect for savouring creative cocktails and soaking up the Barcelona buzz. The hotel has only 20 rooms and suites, all with a very personalised and residential vibe. Think curated artwork, designer furnishings and plush fabrics. Many boast private balconies overlooking the tranquil surrounding streets. Get another wow-view of the city from the rooftop pool and bar, a chic urban oasis where you can unwind after a day of Barcelona adventures, especially when the beach shack Chiringuitos is serving grilled delicacies.

€
From €138 / US$150 for a double room with breakfast.

www.casabonay.com

Stockholm
Embassy District

◆ TO VISIT BEFORE YOU DIE BECAUSE

This is the most unconventional city hotel where elegance and intimacy work like a charm.

A home away from home sounds like a cliché, but, in the case of Et Hem the concept works. This Arts and Crafts-style house has an inviting living room, a kitchen where you can grab a bite to eat and drink, and a cosy library and conservatory next to a patio garden. Owner Jeanette Mix worked closely with Ilse Crawford – the well-known designer of Soho House New York – to create Instagram-worthy interiors. The 12 luxurious and exquisitely furnished bedrooms and suites overlooking the city or the beautiful garden are a joy to return to after a day spent exploring Stockholm.

€€
From €380 / US$425 per night for a double room, with breakfast.

SWEDEN

Gothenburg
City centre

BURLESQUE
BEAUTY

◆ TO VISIT BEFORE YOU DIE BECAUSE

When Gothenburg is snowed under, this hotel is the most intimate retreat in Sweden.

The entire hotel feels like a velvet embrace, a warm nest of explosive patterns and textures, opulent and invigorating, cosseting and inviting. Hotel Pigalle is by far one of the most romantic boutique hotels in Europe for lovers of the boudoir style. All this is in stark contrast to the clean and minimal Scandinavian style of the exterior. The real treat is the breakfast which can be taken while lounging in low sofas next to a real fireplace. In the evening, the space transforms into Restaurant Atelier with an inventive, tasty cuisine and lively cocktail bar. Downstairs, the cosy Bar Amuse serves fine cheese and cold cuts in the evening.

€
From €110 / US$125 per night for a double room, with breakfast.

www.hotelpigalle.se

SWEDEN

Lapland
Harads

TREE MAGIC

◆ TO VISIT BEFORE YOU DIE BECAUSE
Every treehouse should have the look and feel of this fairy-tale-like hotel in a Lappish winter wonderland.

Forget the Icehotel, which is so passé. Choose the Treehotel, a much more exciting option in the wilds of Swedish Lapland, just south of the Arctic Circle. The hotel is made up of seven extraordinary treehouses, each one designed by a different architect and scattered throughout a snow-dusted pine forest. Three of the Treehotel rooms are The Mirrorcube, a glistening glass box with mirrored walls that reflect the surroundings; The Cabin, an organically shaped lookout with large windows;

and The Bird's Nest, an intimate cocoon surrounded by giant twigs and accessed via a retractable ladder. If you're lucky, you might see the Northern Lights dancing above the nearby Lüle River. Hearty meals are served at the traditional Treehotel guesthouse (which also houses cheaper rooms), a short and magical stroll away from the treehouses.

€
From €90 / US$100 per night for a double room, with breakfast.

— 128 —
BELLEVUE DES ALPES

SWITZERLAND

Bernese Oberland
Kleine Scheidegg

THE GREAT
WHITE ESCAPE

◆ TO VISIT BEFORE YOU DIE BECAUSE

This mountain gem with breathtaking vistas of the three highest
mountains in the Swiss Alps is the perfect getaway.

Hop on a tiny mountain train to reach the historic Hotel Bellevue des Alpes, one of the most iconic inns in Switzerland. Cuddle up in one of the 50 historic – but totally renovated – rooms and watch snow clouds gather around the legendary Eiger and Jungfrau mountains outside your window. Enter through the hotel's revolving doors and you will feel like you have been transported back in time. There is a creaky, winding staircase up to the cosy rooms, the corridors lined with old photographs which tell the story of the hotel and the alpinist pioneers who once stayed here. There is neither a sauna nor a spa, so instead have a hot bath before going for an aperitif in the bar, followed by a four-course dinner served on antique silverware and vintage Victorian-style porcelain while looking out onto the legendary north face of the Eiger.

€€
From €355 / US$400 per night for a double room, half board.

212   www.scheidegg-hotels.ch

7132 HOUSE OF ARCHITECTS

| SWITZERLAND | **Graubünden** | UNTOUCHED AND |
| | Vals | PRESERVED |

◆ TO VISIT BEFORE YOU DIE BECAUSE

This is the ultimate design hotel in the European Alps put together by the some of the brightest stars in modern architecture.

Stay in a Pritzker Prize hotel room, designed by world-class architects Peter Zumthor, Tadao Ando, Thom Mayne and Kengo Kuma and internationally awarded for innovative architecture. Each of these starchitects designed the rooms and suites of this hotel in their own individual style. Besides the unique interior design, another reason to stay here in the quaint village of Vals is the legendary thermal baths designed by Peter Zumthor and accessible from this hotel. All 73 rooms and suites in this minimalist masterpiece, surrounded by towering peaks, are all tastefully furnished, including Ando's room which pays tribute to the aesthetics of the Japanese teahouse and Mayne's retreat in local quartzite with a glass-shower centrepiece. For hungry hearts after a day at Therme Vals there are three gourmet restaurants, including the 7132 Silver run by chef Mitja Birlo, which boasts two Michelin stars and 17 Gault Millau points.

€€
From €280 / US$315 per night with breakfast.

www.7132.com

THE NETHERLANDS

Amsterdam
Museumplein

MUSEUM-
WORTHY VIEWS

◆ TO VISIT BEFORE YOU DIE BECAUSE

This 19th-century landmark knows how to play it cool in the 21st century.

Amsterdam has many luxury hotels but the Conservatorium is by far the most stunning place to stay. Hidden in a grand, austere-looking building in the centre of the city, the 129-room hotel designed by Piero Lissoni has beautiful and super-cosy guestrooms and suites, many with striking views of the city centre. Each of the I Love Amsterdam Suites have a rooftop terrace, and Suite 528 looks out onto the Stedelijk Museum through floor-to-ceiling glass. The public areas, bar and restaurants offer some of the city's best food and drink experiences, and the nightclub, which features a DJ on Thursdays, attracts more Amsterdamers than tourists.

€€€
From €440 / US$495 per night for a double room.

THE NETHERLANDS

Amsterdam
City-wide

**NAUTICAL
DREAMS**

◆ TO VISIT BEFORE YOU DIE BECAUSE
This is Amsterdam's most original hotel concept, perfect for the
non-conformist traveller.

There is nothing standard or ordinary
about staying at one of the 28 rooms
that form the Sweets Hotel concept.
All the rooms are former bridge houses
scattered around the city, which have been
transformed into hotel suites, each one
different in style, architecture, location
and size. Some of the rooms are located
in the bustling heart of Amsterdam
Central and are tiny and designed in a
contemporary style, while others are
located with views over a quiet lake
and are build in a more rustic style. The
Amstelschutsluis house is only accessible
by boat, adding to the romance, especially
as the morning breakfast basket has to be
brought over by water, too.

€
From €120 / US$135 per night for a double room.

— 132 —
DE DURGERDAM

◆ TO VISIT BEFORE YOU DIE BECAUSE

This is the new style of small and intimate countryside inns for a real getaway.

This is a truly tranquil and wonderfully green escape away from the crowds, just a 30-minute bike ride from the busy centre of Amsterdam. De Durgerdam is a revitalised 17th-century inn nestled in a charming fishing village of the same name. The inn has 14 super dreamy rooms with a blend of vintage finds and custom-made furniture, featuring Hypnos beds decorated with stunning, locally crafted tulipwood headboards. At this inn natural light plays a key role, reminiscent of

Vermeer's golden age paintings inside, and outside on the stunning terrace with views over the water. On the ground floor is De Mark, a relaxed open-plan restaurant – with a focus on veggies – which is also popular with locals. Think crackling wood-fired stoves, a welcoming bar, and doors opening onto a terrace overlooking the glistening IJmeer lake.

€€
From €302 / US$328 per night for a double room
with breakfast.

www.dedurgerdam.com

| UK | London | COUTURE |
| | Kensington | STYLE |

◆ TO VISIT BEFORE YOU DIE BECAUSE

This is probably London's first true boutique hotel and still retains its eccentric charm and high style.

Designed and styled by former Bond girl Anouska Hempel, this iconic Kensington couture hotel is a world of bohemian cosiness and warmth. Behind the black Victorian brick walls, you'll find a provocative fusion of Eastern and Western decors and styles – an eclectic mix of shiny mirrors, walnut tones and cosy bedrooms. Blakes Restaurant and Blakes Below Bar attract movie stars, musicians and designers, and the Matthew Williamson-designed courtyard hideaway with its lush palm trees, Moroccan-tiled flooring and wrought-iron tables dressed in tropical-print tablecloths is the ideal spot to relax and sip a cocktail.

€€
From €350 / US$390 per night for a double room.

— 134 —
THE BLOOMSBURY

UK

London
Bloomsbury

ULTIMATE URBAN
HIDEAWAY

◆ TO VISIT BEFORE YOU DIE BECAUSE

This hotel has the coolest bedrooms and the cosiest cocktail bar in London.

The Bloomsbury Hotel, close to Tottenham Court Road and the busy shopping streets of central London, is housed in a striking red-brick Sir Edwin Lutyens building dating from 1928. Despite its boutique feel, the hotel has 153 rooms and 11 suites in gorgeous modern art deco style with lots of lush velvet, Mid-Century Modern chairs and amazing beds. Downstairs, you should head for the Coral Room in the evening to try one of the 30-plus English sparkling wines or a perfectly presented cocktail. There's also a pleasant terrace for summery days where a hearty breakfast or a casual lunch and dinner is served.

€€
From €295 / US$330 per night for a double room, with breakfast.

FOUR SEASONS PARK LANE

UK	London	CLASSIC
	Mayfair	ELEGANCE

◆ TO VISIT BEFORE YOU DIE BECAUSE

This is true Mayfair classic chic with the best and most personal service in the UK capital.

The Four Seasons Park Lane has an impressive CV: this is the oldest Four Seasons in Europe, opened in 1970 and still one of the best luxury hotels in London. It's the ultimate urban refuge offering timeless elegance and extremely comfortable rooms (some with terraces) looking out over Park Lane. The interior was recently given a facelift by renowned designer Pierre-Yves Rochon, and the retro art deco vibe in the uber-cosy lounge bar is just perfect. One of those magical places in town where you can grab breakfast in a small garden on a sunny day.

€€€
From €650 / US$730 per night for a double room, with breakfast.

www.fourseasons.com/london

HECKFIELD PLACE

UK	Hampshire	SLOW
	Hook	BEAUTY

◆ TO VISIT BEFORE YOU DIE BECAUSE

This is the smartest country house hotel in England, just an hour's journey away from busy London.

This red-brick Georgian manor dating back to 1790 stands as a beacon of warmth and rural chic amid some 160 hectares (150 acres) of finely manicured gardens surrounded by woodlands and ancient walnut and birch trees. The interior decor is one to embrace on a cold, wintery day when all the open fires in the main house are lit and high tea is served in the sun-filled Morning Room. Head designer Ben Thompson, a protégé of Ilse Crawford, focused on raw and artisanal materials: pure Irish linen has natural timbers and matting woven from sweet-smelling River Ouse rush. Some of the 45 bedrooms are in the main house, while others are located in the new wing and have a more urban feel, with bedrooms that flow seamlessly into the cosy sitting area. The hotel's two restaurants, Marle and Hearth, are overseen by Australian chef Skye Gyngell. Marle serves inventive and seasonal à la carte dishes, while Hearth with its huge fireplace is a more rustic affair, reserved for hotel guests only.

€€
From €350 / US$390 per night for a double room, with breakfast.

— 137 —
KINLOCH LODGE

UK

Scotland
Isle of Skye

ATLANTIC
ROMANCE

◆ TO VISIT BEFORE YOU DIE BECAUSE

Kinloch Lodge creates a true home from home for its guests offering unparalleled Scottish hospitality.

This historic hotel was recently completely refurbished to give the place a fresher and more contemporary look and feel. Despite its updated style, portraits dating back to the time of the exiled Stuart king still adorn the walls of this elegant 16th-century country house. The rooms are uber-romantic with beds you want to crawl into after a long walk on the remote island of Skye. Enjoy an energizing breakfast of topped with a perfectly poached egg. When a storm rolls in from the Atlantic there are plenty of roaring fires to keep you warm as you look out over the soothing shoreline of Loch na Dal.

€€
From €250 / US$280 per night for a double room, with breakfast.

— 138 —
THE FIFE ARMS

UK

Scottish Highlands
Braemar

WILD
ROMANCE

◆ TO VISIT BEFORE YOU DIE BECAUSE

Staying here is like reading a romantic Scottish novel that you never want to put down.

There is no other place in Scotland where Scottish tradition meets the best of contemporary, international art. A stay at this fascinating passion project from international art dealers Hauser & Wirth, is like stepping into another world. Interior designer Russell Sage has used lavish textiles, a wealth of antiques and fine oriental rugs, while converting high-style decorative elements into luxurious objets d'art. The 46 rooms and suites have different themes, ranging from

Scottish Culture to Nature and Poetry, all looking out over the dramatic Highlands. Downstairs is the Flying Stag, the hotel's public bar, where you can rub shoulders with the locals, and Elsa's Bar, where you can drink champagne and cocktails before digging into smoked oysters or a piece of Highland beef cooked over the fire.

€€
From €250 / US$272 per night for a double room, with breakfast.

KILLIEHUNTLY FARMHOUSE

| UK | **Scottish Highlands**
Cairngorms National Park | ATLANTIC
ROMANCE |

◆ TO VISIT BEFORE YOU DIE BECAUSE

This wonderfully creative farmhouse is a true Scottish island escape, not to be missed.

Killiehuntly's Danish owners have converted this 17th-century farmhouse, located on almost 1,600 hectares (4,000 acres) of private land, into one of the most romantic hotels in Scotland. Just a stone's throw from Aviemore in the wilds of the Scottish Highlands, you will find this hideaway wrapped in ultra-cosy, Scandinavian style. There are only four rooms, each named after native trees: Elm, Alder, Birch and Oak. Luxury comes here in alternative forms, so don't except a phone, a minibar or a television. A real treat here is the farm-to-table dining experience with homey and hearty food, just perfect after a long biking or hiking session in the surrounding hills.

€€
From €220 / US$245 per night for a double room, with breakfast.

www.killiehuntly.scot

150 HOTELS YOU NEED TO VISIT BEFORE YOU DIE

— 140 —
RAFFLES LONDON AT THE OWO

UK

London
Whitehall

A LONDON
LEGEND

This is London's newest, most epic hotel with a sensational past.

In 2023, London's historic Whitehall neighbourhood welcomed a dazzling newcomer: Raffles London at The OWO. Housed in the meticulously restored Old War Office (OWO) building, it was once home to legendary figures like Winston Churchill (who famously planned D-Day here) and a hub for British intelligence agencies MI5 and MI6. The challenge was to seamlessly blend contemporary Raffles elegance with the building's rich heritage. The hotel has 120 opulent rooms and suites. Some offer private balconies overlooking this famous neighbourhood where the Houses of Parliament and Downing Street are located. Raffles transforms into a (fine)-dining destination with nine restaurants and bars, from all-day Mediterranean fare to chic cocktail experiences. The most captivating space might be the tiny Spy Bar, hidden in an old interrogation room in the basement, with its red velvet banquettes and a half-car from *No Time to Die* hanging on the wall.

€€€
From €800 / US$871 for a double room with breakfast.

www.raffles.com/london

233

100 PRINCES STREET

UK

Scotland
Edinburgh

EXPLORER
CHIC

◆ TO VISIT BEFORE YOU DIE BECAUSE

This might be Scotland's most romantic urban hotel with a serious explorer's past.

Steeped in history, 100 Princes Street sits right in the heart of darling Edinburgh. Formerly the headquarters of the Royal Over-Seas League, this luxurious hotel dates back to 1933, a time when Scottish explorers once called it home. There are only 19 unique rooms and suites, all decorated with handpicked antiques and custom-made Araminta Campbell tartans. The interior is fabulously romantic with windows offering amazing views of Edinburgh Castle and the iconic Princes Street. After exploring charming Edinburgh, there is a fireplace waiting, perfect for winding down with a glass of whisky at the Ghillie's Pantry bar – you might struggle to choose between the more than 100 references on the shelves – before trying the ultra-romantic The Wallace restaurant serving local classics with an agreeable, refined edge – try the haggis bonbons with a whisky dip.

€€
From €270 / US$294 for a double room with breakfast.

— 142 —
EMPIRE RETREAT

AUSTRALIA | **Margaret River**
Yallingup | ADULTS
ONLY

◆ TO VISIT BEFORE YOU DIE BECAUSE

Hiding away in beautiful Margaret River should be done in a stylish retreat.

Romance is very cool, especially if you stay at this rural retreat built around a farmhouse in the north of Margaret River. Situated among farmland and vineyards, the retreat is all about designer interiors with a focus on local wood, stone and tin roofs. There are 11 romantic suites, including two loft suites in the original farmhouse and three split-level luxury villas with four-poster beds, fireplaces, mini-kitchens, outdoor showers and spa baths. The breakfast is one to wake up for: delicious wood-fired bread with local honey and hearty egg dishes with cold meats.

€
From €150 / US$270 per night for a double room, with breakfast.

www.empireretreat.com

AUSTRALIA

New South Wales
Cabarita Beach

SURFER'S
COOL

◆ TO VISIT BEFORE YOU DIE BECAUSE
This intimate surf hotel will win your heart with its style and ambiance.

This used to be a very simple and cheap surf motel until two Australian sisters transformed it into undoubtedly the most unique five-star boutique hotel in Australia. Past the palm trees is Cabarita Beach, home to one of Australia's best surf breaks and one of the country's most idyllic beachfront villages. Halcyon House is a collage of blue and white that screams water, ocean, surf and holidays. The in-house restaurant, Paper Daisy, has blue-and-white wicker chairs and is a cool place to grab a drink or have a long brunch. All 21 rooms overlook the central swimming pool and have quirky wallpaper, copper lamps and wooden floors. The bathrooms have handmade blue-and-white tiles, gilt-framed mirrors and antique-inspired faucets.

€€
From €360 / US$405 per night for a double room, with breakfast.

AUSTRALIA	**Northern Territory** Uluru	LOCATION LOCATION

◆ TO VISIT BEFORE YOU DIE BECAUSE

A natural wonder like Uluru should be intensely watched from a luxury abode like this hotel.

Longitude 131° is a real bucket-list hotel. It's not cheap, it's remote, it's exclusive, but for those wanting to wake up or fall asleep with panoramic views of the Uluru / Ayers Rock and the Outback in the deep centre of Australia, there is only one hotel that can offer this. Longitude 131° is the closest hotel to Uluru but you are far away from the busy town and busloads of tourists. Each of the 15 suites is a luxury tent on stilts with a wide terrace, a double daybed and an outdoor ecological fireplace. At night, you can watch the stars while sipping a drink and fall asleep next to the roaring fire. The rooms have large windows with screens to protect you from creepy crawlies, so you can leave the windows open when Uluru changes colour and shape as the sun sets and rises.

€€€€
From €2,100 / US$2,355 per night for a double room, all inclusive.

— 145 —
PUMPHOUSE POINT

AUSTRALIA

Tasmania
Lake St Clair

FLOATING
HERITAGE

◆ TO VISIT BEFORE YOU DIE BECAUSE
Quirky Tasmania has become a sought-after destination and this hidden
hotel is an absolute must-stay.

Hidden in an old, five-storey hydro-pump station in Tasmania you will find Pumphouse Point, a new wilderness retreat with theatrical views over Lake St Clair. In the 1940s, hydroelectric turbines occupied this industrial relic. Nowadays, there are 18 elegant bedrooms spread over two buildings: the actual Pump House on the water and the Lake House on the shore. All have floor-to-ceiling windows and a timeless interior designed by the Tasmanian-based architectural company Cumulus Studio. This art deco-style industrial heritage site is the best place to experience and witness Tasmania's wilderness in one stunning and very exceptional location. Even city lovers will enjoy the roaring fire and the amazing views from the bar, which operates on an honour system so you can fix your own favourite cocktail, or taste one of the two locally distilled whiskies.

€
From €180 / US$200 per night for a double room, with breakfast.

AUSTRALIA	New South Wales	SADDLE-UP
	Byron Bay	ESCAPE

◆ TO VISIT BEFORE YOU DIE BECAUSE

This ranch Down Under is all about maximalist fun and true escapism.

Surf the waves in darling Byron Bay, then head inland to stay at one of Australia's coolest hotels. The Byron hinterland is buzzing after the opening of Sun Ranch in 2023: a secluded paradise spread over 23 hectares of rolling green hills. The hotel is owned by fashionista Jamie Blakey and local restaurateur Julia Ashwood, who have really thrown out the rustic ranch rulebook. The result is a maximalist explosion of colour, pattern and texture with lots of azure and flamingo, swirling terracotta floors, plush velvet lounges and dazzling beaded chandeliers. There are a total of 17 very different rooms and suites, with four guest rooms and a private pool in the Rambler House. You can go horse riding (of course), but also cruise around on electric bikes, play games on the vintage badminton court, and relax in the Cowboy Bar (while sipping chilli-infused tequilas) or sexy Pool Club with wood-fired sauna and even an ice bath. Al fresco lunches, prepared on an open fire, Argentinean style, are served at the Field House.

€€
From €350 / US$381 for a double room with breakfast.

www.sunranch.com.au

— 147 —
FOUR SEASONS RESORT BORA BORA

FRENCH
POLYNESIA

Bora Bora
North side of the lagoon

LAGOON
LIFE

◆ TO VISIT BEFORE YOU DIE BECAUSE

This honeymoon Valhalla is the most perfect and beautiful resort in
the intensely blue Pacific.

For fans of swimming pool-style, emerald-hued water and overwater bungalows, this is by far the best luxury hotel in the whole of the Pacific. Opened in 2008, this Four Seasons is still in a league of its own, delivering not only perfect views over the blue lagoon and the mountains in the distance, but also perfect service and beautiful design. The many white beaches and manicured gardens are faultlessly maintained and the 100 overwater bungalows are the best in French Polynesia. They all come with a spacious living room, outdoor deck with shower, snorkel gear, and a large bathtub for two. For families and friends there are seven beachfront villas with two or three bedrooms.

€€€
From €700 / US$785 per night for a double room,
with breakfast.

www.fourseasons.com/borabora

COMO LAUCALA ISLAND

SOUTH PACIFIC	Fiji	BLUE BULL
	Laucala Island	

◆ TO VISIT BEFORE YOU DIE BECAUSE

This is one of the most exclusive private islands and offers a taste of the Pacific in true Fiji style.

This private island sanctuary of Red Bull co-founder, Dietrich Mateschitz, is as a blue lagoon as you can get: endless stretches of private forest and coconut groves, interwoven with a golf course, several swimming pools, waterfalls and surrounded by the deep-blue Pacific. There are just 25 villas, ranging from forest hideaways to beachside boudoirs, all with a pool, outdoor shower and lots of private living space. The minibar is packed with (complimentary) drinks including Red Bull, Carpe Diem kombucha, champagne and beers. The decor is Fijian tropical with thatched roofs and large windows and features many local materials in the form of wood, palm leaves and seashells.

€€
From €2,300 / US$2,580 per night for a double room, all inclusive.

NEW ZEALAND	**North Island** Lake Taupo	WILD ELEGANCE

◆ TO VISIT BEFORE YOU DIE BECAUSE

Even after all these years, this is still the number-one luxury hotel in New-Zealand.

Big-name politicians and Hollywood stars have stayed here to hide away from the world, surrounded by lush green grounds, next to the fast-flowing Waikato River and the famous Huka Falls. Despite the fact that many other luxury lodges have opened in New Zealand, Huka Lodge remains the leading lady. You can linger for hours in the public areas which are stocked with antique furniture, portraits, Maori artefacts and objets d'art collected from around the world. The style is 'a rainy day in Scotland' with lots of tartan carpets and deep colours. The rooms have bi-folding doors that open onto the riverside where quacking ducks pass by, and if you want to fall asleep to the sound of the water, the mosquito netting will protect you from getting bitten. Gastronomy is heavenly at Huka Lodge with romantic candlelit dinners and amazing local wines.

€€€
From €850 / US$955 per night for a double room, all inclusive.

THE LINDIS

| NEW ZEALAND | South Island | HIDDEN |
| | Ahuriri Valley | LUXURY |

◆ TO VISIT BEFORE YOU DIE BECAUSE

This luxury lodge surrounded by pristine wilderness is the ideal getaway
from everyday life.

This stunning lodge blends like no other into its surroundings with the roof shape following the natural curves of the land, creating a sense of belonging to the landscape. It's all about using natural rock and timber, plus elegant furniture and artwork, to create an inviting place to stay. The Lindis has five suites, and not far from the main lodge are the new luxury mirrored pods, offering immense views over the rugged landscape and coast. The style and ambiance are both relaxed and sophisticated, with the focus on the 2,500 hectares (2,200 acres) or so of private land surrounding the lodge. Here guests can indulge in horse riding, fly fishing or even gliding through the air in little planes.

€€€
From €1,100 / US$1,235 per night for a double room, all inclusive.

INDEX

PHOTO CREDITS

Hotel 01: stock image, Elsa Young / Hotel 02: stock image Migrante Guesthouse / Hotel 03: Fabrice Rampert / Hotel 04: stock image Kinondo Kwetu / Hotel 05: Alan Keohane / Hotel 07: Andrew Montgomery / Hotel 08: stock image, wilderness safari / Hotel 09: / Hotel 10: Singita Kwitonda Lodge / Hotel 11: Jean Luke Payet / Hotel 12: stock images Hilton International / Hotel 13: Dookphoto. com / Hotel 14: stock images Natural Selection / Hotel 15: Dookphoto.com / Hotel 16: sterrekopjes / Hotel 17: Beyond Grumeti Serengeti River Lodge / Hotel 18: Dookphoto.com / Hotel 19: Paul Karnstedt Photography / Hotel 21: stock image Kempinski Hotels / Hotel 22: stock image Goldeneye / Hotel 23: stock image Jade Mountain / Hotel 24: Alex Fradkin / Hotel 26: Manbir Sehmi / Hotel 27: Jeremy Koresi / Hotel 30: stock images The Ludlow / Hotel 32: stock image House of Jasmines / Hotel 33: stock image Estancia Rincon / Hotel 34: Palacio Duhau / Hotel 35: stock images Belmond Hotels / Hotel 36: Tarso Figueira / Hotel 37: stock images Explora Hotels / Hotel 38: stock images Tierra Hotels / Hotel 39: AM LOPEZ / Hotel 41: Jorge Chagas & Susie Elberse (left & bottom right), Marcos Guiponi (top right) / Hotel 42: stock images Gangtey Lodge / Hotel 43: John McDermott and Aman Resorts Limited / Hotel 44: stock image Knai Bang Chatt / Hotel 45: stock images Banyan Tree Resorts / Hotel 46: stock images Hyatt Hotels / Hotel 47: stock images Mandarin Hotels / Hotel 48: Steve Turvey / Hotel 49: Guy Hervais and Taj Hotels / Hotel 50: birdworld / Hotel 51: stock image Raas Hotels / Hotel 52: stock image Nihi Sumba / Hotel 53: Hoshinoya Bali / Hotel 56: stock image Mandarin Oriental Hotels / Hotel 57: stock image Hyatt Hotels / Hotel 58: Miles & Miles LLC / Hotel 59: Jonathan Perugia and Inle Princess Resort / Hotel 60: stock image Peacock Guesthouse / Hotel 61: The Happy House / Hotel 62: Shinta Mani / Hotel 63: stock images Alila Hotels / Hotel 64: Tanveer Badal (top left & right), Erika Hobart / Hotel 65: Tooten, Accor Hotels / Hotel 66: ML Spencer, Aman Resorts / Hotel 67: Kaju Green / Hotel 68: John W. McDermott, Miles & Miles LLC / Hotel 69: Simon Birt / Hotel 70: Adam Bruzzone / Hotel 71: stock image Azerai / Hotel 74: guenterstandl.de / Hotel 76: Robert Rieger / Hotel 77: stock image Van Cleef Hotel / Hotel 78: stock image Hotel Nordlandet / Hotel 79: stock image Radisson Blu Hotel / Hotel 82: Teemu Kiiskinen / Hotel 83: Benoit Linero / Hotel 84: stock image La Divine Comédie / Hotel 85: L. Di Orio / Hotel 86: Lily of the Valley / Hotel 87: Maison Proust / Hotel 88: stock image Hotel Kazbegi / Hotel 89: stock image Das Stue Hotel / Hotel 90: stock image Schloss Elmau / Hotel 91: Phaea Blue Palace / Hotel 92: Monument Hotel / Hotel 93: Myrto Iatropoulou / Hotel 94: Verina / Hotel 95: Lisa Burns, Gustav Thuesen for World of Greenland / Hotel 98: stock images Deplar Farm / Hotel 100: The Retreat at Blue Lagoon / Hotel 101: Jack Hard / Hotel 102: stock image Breac.House / Hotel 103: stock image Il San Pietro / Hotel 104: Kate Martin / Hotel 105: Gundolf Pfotenhauer / Hotel 107: Il Monastero / Hotel 108: Romazzino / Hotel 109: Susafa / Hotel 111: Ramon Lucas / Hotel 113: Wolf Lodge / Hotel 114: Fabrice Demoullin / Hotel 115: stock images Casa de Sao Lourenco / Hotel 118: stock image Palacio Verride / Hotel 119: Four Seasons Hotel Lisbon / Hotel 122: stock image Sant Francesc / Hotel 123: stock images Marbella Club / Hotel 124: Casa Bonay / Hotel 125: stock image Et Hemm / Hotel 126: stock image Hotel Pigalle / Hotel 127: stock image Tree Hotel / Hotel 128: stock images Hotel Bellevue des Alpes / Hotel 129: Global Image Creation – 7132 Hotel, Hotel Vals / Hotel 130: stock image Conservatorium Hotel / Hotel 131: Mirjam Bleeker and Sweets Hotel / Hotel 132: Studio Unfolded / Hotel 133: Timothy Atkins / Hotel 134: stock image The Doyle Collection / Hotel 135: stock image Four Seasons Hotel / Hotel 136: stock images Heckfield Place / Hotel 137: Helen Cathcart / Hotel 138: Simphotography / Hotel 139: Martin Kaufman / Hotel 140: Raffles London at the OWO / Hotel 141: 100 Princes Street / Hotel 143: Kara Rosenlund / Hotel 144: George Apostolidis / Hotel 145: Adam Gibson / Hotel 146: Sun Ranch / Hotel 148: stock image Laucala Island Resort / Hotel 150: stock images The Lindis

150 | SPAS | YOU NEED TO VISIT BEFORE YOU DIE

150 | VINEYARDS | YOU NEED TO VISIT BEFORE YOU DIE

150 | BOOKSTORES | YOU NEED TO VISIT BEFORE YOU DIE

150 | GARDENS | YOU NEED TO VISIT BEFORE YOU DIE

150 | BARS | YOU NEED TO VISIT BEFORE YOU DIE

150 | RESTAURANTS | YOU NEED TO VISIT BEFORE YOU DIE

150 | WINE BARS | YOU NEED TO VISIT BEFORE YOU DIE

150 | HOUSES | YOU NEED TO VISIT BEFORE YOU DIE

150 | GOLF COURSES | YOU NEED TO VISIT BEFORE YOU DIE

150 | HOTELS | YOU NEED TO VISIT BEFORE YOU DIE

IN THE SAME
— SERIES —

150 spas you need to visit before you die
isbn 978 94 014 9747 3

—

150 vineyards you need to visit before you die
isbn 978 94 014 8546 3

—

150 bookstores you need to visit before you die
isbn 978 94 014 8935 5

—

150 gardens you need to visit before you die
isbn 978 94 014 7929 5

—

150 bars you need to visit before you die
isbn 978 94 014 4912 0

—

150 wine bars you need to visit before you die
isbn 978 94 014 8622 4

—

150 houses you need to visit before you die
isbn 978 94 014 6204 4

—

150 golf courses you need to visit before you die
isbn 978 94 014 8195 3

—

150 restaurants you need to visit before you die
isbn 978 94 014 9570 7

—

150 national parks you need to visit before you die
isbn 978 94 014 1970 3

Colophon

All Texts
Debbie Pappyn - www.classetouriste.be

Copy-editing
Melanie Shapiro
Heather Sills

All images (except see p. 255)
David De Vleeschauwer - www.classetouriste.be

Back Cover Image:
Steve Turvey

Book Design
ASB

Typesetting
Keppie & Keppie

If you have any questions or comments about
the material in this book, please do not hesitate
to contact our editorial team: art@lannoo.com

© Lannoo Publishers, Belgium, 2024
NUR 504/500
ISBN 978 94 014 3022 7

www.lannoo.com

All rights reserved. No part of this publication may
be reproduced or transmitted in any form or by any
means, electronic or mechanical, including photocopy,
recording or any other information storage and
retrieval system, without prior permission in writing
from the publisher.

Every effort bas been made to trace copyright bolders.
If, however, you feel that you have inadvertently been
overlooked, please contact the publishers.